D0504670

WITHDRAWN FROM HAVERING COLLEGES
SIXTH FORM LIBRARY

THROWING

796.43

42334

THROWING

MAX JONES

British Amateur Athletic Board

HAVERING SIXTH FORM
COLLEGE Wingletye Lane, Hornchurch,
RM11 3TB. ☎ 01 08 610962

THE CROWOOD PRESS

First published in 1987 by
THE CROWOOD PRESS
Ramsbury, Marlborough,
Wiltshire SN8 2HE

© BAAB 1987

All rights reserved. No part of this publication may be reproduced
or transmitted in any form or by any means, electronic or
mechanical, including photocopy, recording or any information
storage and retrieval system without permission in writing from the
publishers.

British Library Cataloguing in Publication Data

Jones, Max
  Throwing.
  1. Weight throwing
  I. Title
  796.4'35   GV1093

  ISBN 0-946284-09-1

Dedicated to my wife Barbara, for her help and encouragement.

Acknowledgements

Line illustrations by Annette Findlay

Figs 121, 122, 124, 160 to 162, 189 to 193 by the author. All other
photographs by Howard Payne.

Cover photographs courtesy of Mark Shearman.

Series Adviser David Bunker, Lecturer, Loughborough University
of Technology

Typeset by Q Set, Gloucester
Printed in Great Britain

Contents

Max Jones is a BAAB National Coach and the Chief Coach for Throws in Great Britain. He qualified as a Senior Coach at the age of 22 and has subsequently coached international athletes in all four disciplines. He was Team Coach at the 1983 World Championships, 1984 Olympics and the 1986 European Championships, as well as being Chief Coach for the England Men's team at the 1986 Commonwealth Games.

Max Jones has most successfully drawn on his experience as athlete, teacher and coach to produce an outstanding book on the four throwing events. Technique, training and programme planning are discussed thoughtfully and sensitively. This at once renders the complex simple – an achievement which few authors on throws have come close to – and brings into sharp focus a comprehensive fund of interesting information.

This is the best book on throws I have read, making these events come alive as exciting challenges which can be well met with thoughtful interpretation of Max's advice. It is a meaningful read for athletes, teachers and coaches, and the expertise of the author, Chief Throws Coach for the British Amateur Athletic Board, lends immense weight to the text.

Frank W. Dick
Director of Coaching
British Amateur Athletic Board

Exponents of the throwing events are commonly known as 'The Heavies', and Max Jones's close association as coach to some of the best of this rare breed has given him a vast knowledge of the four disciplines. His excellent ability to communicate as a coach has been transferred into an easily understandable text, that includes the vital points of technique and preparation relevant to today's coach and athlete.

Pure ability and dedication are just not enough to succeed in today's throwing events. Another component is needed, that of 'contemporary knowledge'. Max cannot supply the two former components, but he has given everyone the opportunity to have the latter at their fingertips.

David Ottley

Introduction

Over the years styles of throwing may change but the basic fundamentals of the four throwing events do not. In this book I have purposely avoided taking an in depth look at the finer points of event technique, concentrating instead on the basic skills that all elite throwers possess. It is far too easy to perceive throwing events as complicated and highly technical; indeed, this belief has frightened away many potential coaches. The dominant technical points are, in fact, simple and easily learned and retained. It is essential that young throwers quickly acquire these basic skills as the solid foundation of their training.

Throwing has improved enormously over the past two decades and top performers at home and overseas are achieving huge distances. A world-class athlete launching an implement far into the distance is an exciting spectacle. Such expertise does not come easily; years of hard and patient work are needed to attain the highest levels of skill and power. Gone are the days when good performances could be achieved with poor technique or without dedication.

The young athlete will no doubt be introduced to the sport at school and will graduate to the local athletics club. Despite Britain's well-organised coaching scheme, there is a shortage of field event coaches. If the local club has a good throwing coach, he will be easily recognised by the athletes he produces and by his reputation. Where no specialist coach exists, this book should bridge the gap. If you are a club coach, you will find information to help you coach the throwing events; if you are an athlete, you will soon be able to introduce yourself to throwing.

Note This book is written for right-handed throwers. Left-handed throwers should substitute right for left and vice versa.

1 Fundamentals of Throwing

BASIC FORMULA

The four throwing events may involve different techniques but all share some fundamental principles. Whether you are an athlete or a coach, you should be aware of these so that you can apply them to each of the throwing events. The formula common to all is :

Distance Thrown = Range (Time) × Force

This formula produces the implement's velocity as it leaves the hand; velocity makes the most important contribution to the overall distance thrown.

Force

This is a combination of the athlete's own strength and speed which is applied to the implement during a throw. A thrower's force can be improved by increasing his strength and/or by improving his co-ordination.

Range

However much force a thrower exerts, if he applies it over only a short period of time and distance, the implement will not travel very far. Many hours spent on improving technique will enable the thrower to apply his force over as great a range as possible and to co-ordinate his muscles to produce their maximum efficiency.

Basic Mechanics

Three mechanical factors influence the distance achieved although they are less decisive than force and range.

Angle of Release (Fig 1)

The implement is released at an angle to the ground. If the implement was fired from a cannon at ground level, the perfect angle of release would be 45 degrees. However, throwing implements are all released above ground level, so the perfect angle is

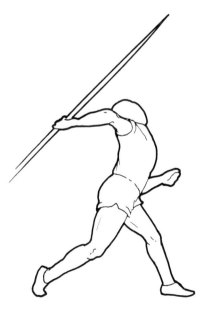

Fig 1   *Good technique will ensure correct angle of release.*

less than 45 degrees. Do not be too concerned about release angle, since good technique will ensure that it is correct.

Height of Release (Fig 2)

Always try to release the implement as high as possible. This will gain the extra centimetres that could win you the competition. Again, sound technique will ensure that optimum height is achieved.

Aerodynamic Factors (Fig 3)

These, of course, do not apply to the shot or hammer as they are both round, non-aerodynamic objects. In the javelin and discus events, however, this is a vital factor which can add many metres to the distance thrown. Both implements must be angled to the air flow so that they experience the aerodynamic forces which aid their flight.

Fig 2   The implement should be released as high as possible.

As small a surface area as possible should be presented to the oncoming air flow. Angling the discus or javelin too high will result in stalling and poor distances.

Fundamental Principles

Bearing in mind the basic formula and mechanics of throwing, you will further maximise your potential by following some fundamental principles.

Slow to Fast (Figs 4 to 8)

Look at any good thrower and observe that he will start his throw slowly and finish it fast, whether using a circle or, in the case of javelin, a runway. The only point where speed is of vital importance is at the moment of release when the implement must be moving as fast as possible. The whole throw is a gradual build-up to this explosive release. Many youngsters make the mistake of beginning too fast and being forced to slow down in mid-throw. 'Start slow, finish fast' is common to all throwing events.

Summation of Forces

This mechanical principle is linked to the 'slow to fast' idea. The strongest muscles of the body, in the thighs and lower back, move heavy objects efficiently and should be used at the start of the throw, to make the implement accelerate from zero to a high speed. Once the implement is moving quickly, the weaker but faster moving muscle groups in shoulders and arms can add speed to an already fast moving object. The muscle groups must therefore be used in sequence – leg and back muscles first, torso and arms last. The record-breaking thrower is like a firework display; ankle

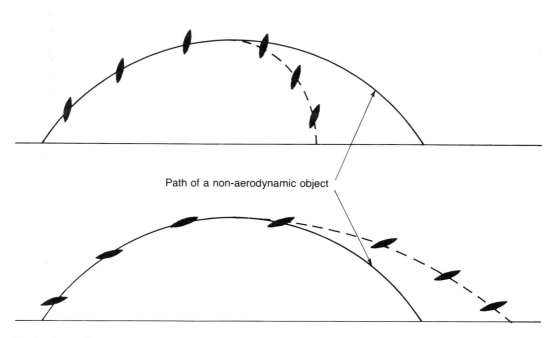

Path of a non-aerodynamic object

Fig 3 As small a surface area as possible should be presented to the oncoming air flow.

explodes, calf explodes, thigh, hip, back, chest, deltoid, arm and finally fingers all explode in sequence, each generating and adding speed to the throw. The old adage 'arm fast and last' is a good one.

Low to High (Figs 4 & 8)

You should always start in a low position and finish high. The low initial position is achieved by bending your legs, allowing those large, powerful muscles to be used over a great range. A high initial position would mean a small range with only the muscles of the upper body being utilised.

Left Side Brace (Figs 7 & 8)

To finish high, the right-handed thrower must brace his left, non-throwing side. A braced left side is essential if the active

right side is to accelerate around it. Without this solid support, the amount of force generated would be severely restricted. You should develop this ability to resist with your non-throwing side early in your career.

Legs Dominant

Your potential is not judged by your strong biceps but by how athletic and powerful your legs are. In all throwing, the legs dictate and dominate; much time and effort must be spent realising their potential in terms of skill and explosive strength.

Balance

No matter how strong you are, you must adopt a balanced position in order to exert your strength. No one can be strong in an unbalanced position. A good technique will

Fig 4   Wolfgang Schmidt (GDR), former world record holder and Olympic medallist, showing a low starting position.

Fig 5   A balanced entry position.

Fig 6   The power position.

Fig 7   An active right side of the body accelerating around a braced left side.

Fig 8   Finishing the throw tall and fast.

develop balance points at the rear of the throw, mid-throw (*Figs 5 & 6*) and at the end. Balance comes from many hours of skill training.

Rhythm

Rhythm is a slightly more elusive concept to grasp but if you watch top-class performers, the rhythm of the movement will become obvious. Although the 'slow to fast' principle holds good, it is not a true linear acceleration but an undulating acceleration. The best advice is that the power position must not be rushed. Here the body's forces gather before the final, tremendously explosive throw. Rhythm comes from learning to feel the tempo of the throw in practice. Relax and feel its ebb and flow.

2 The Shot

Putting the shot is the simplest of the throwing events and is dominated at the highest levels by big, strong, heavy athletes. However, don't assume that great size and strength are the only qualities required. A successful shot putter must be skilful, fast and explosive – in short, an *athlete*. At school levels the skilful and strong boy or girl of only average build can compete with success by mastering the technique of throwing and training consistently.

RULES (*Fig 9*)

The shot is put from a circle 2·135m in diameter, with a wooden stop board 10cm high at its front edge. The athlete must start from a stationary position and, after completing the throw, must leave the circle from the rear half. The shot must be put from one hand and must be close to the chin at the start of the throw. The shot must land within a sector of 40 degrees and the distance is

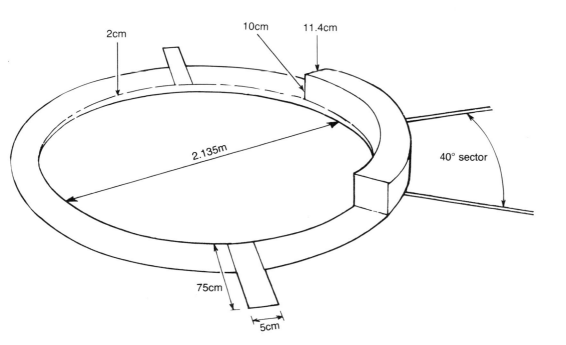

2cm   10cm   11.4cm

2.135m

40° sector

75cm

5cm

Fig 9   The shot put circle.

13

measured from the landing point closest to the circle.

	Men	**Women**
Colt* (U–13)	3·25kg	2·75kg
Junior (U–15)	4kg	3·25kg
Intermediate (U–17)	5kg	4kg
Euro Junior	(U–20)	(U–19)
	6·25kg	4kg
Senior	7·26kg	4kg
*recommended		

Fig 10 The competitive weights for shot putting.

LEARNING TO SHOT PUT

The table giving competitive weights for shot putting should be ignored by those learning the event. Select an implement that feels comfortable to handle, not too heavy but not too light.

Grip (Figs 11 & 12)

In all throwing events the first essential to be learned is the grip. No matter how good

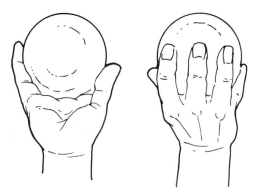

Fig 11 The correct shot put grip.

your technique is, if your grip is incorrect, the shot will not travel far and injury to your fingers could result.

The shot should be placed at the base of the first three fingers, evenly spread, with the little finger and thumb supporting. The shot is then placed under, or next to, the chin with the elbow held high.

Fig 12 The shot correctly positioned with a high elbow.

Basic Throw (Fig 13)

Having established the correct grip, it should be tested out in the simplest throwing position possible. Face the direction of the throw with both feet facing in that direction. Put the shot without using any leg or torso movement, ensuring that the throwing elbow is kept high. Once confident of the grip, you can bend both legs and twist your torso to give greater impetus to the shot.

Standing Throw (Figs 14 & 15)

The standing throw position, or power position, accounts for 90 per cent of the

Fig 13   Standing frontal put, using legs.

Fig 14   The standing throw.

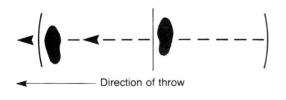

Direction of throw

Fig 15   Foot positions for the standing throw.

distance thrown. Stand sideways with your shoulders square to the rear. The width of the stance will vary according to your leg length but will be between 80 and 90cm. The front foot should be slightly out of line with the direction of the throw. Concentrate on the left toe being opposite the right instep. The standing position should result in chin, knee and toe being vertically in line.

From the chin–knee–toe position the movement starts with the right leg pushing the hips forward over the front foot. The elbow should be kept behind the shot and the arm is used 'fast and last' after the leg, hips and back muscles have completed their movement. The non-throwing side of the body should be kept rigid and tall as the arm strikes.

Using the Circle (Fig 16)

Having mastered the standing throw, you should use the full diameter of the circle by simply shuffling across it. This will add extra distance to your throw. Whichever method you use to add momentum, you

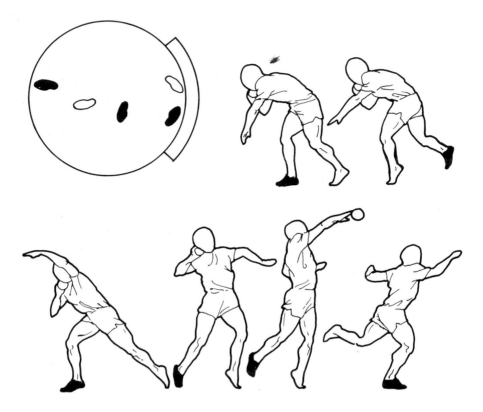

Fig 16 Using the circle to add momentum.

should always ensure that the chin–knee–toe position is assumed before the put is made.

The Glide (Fig 17)

If your maximum potential is to be realised, you must learn to glide (or hop) across the circle. This requires a lot of practice if you are to arrive at the end of a three foot hop in a balanced chin–knee–toe position. The best method of learning a low, balanced backward hop is to perform multiple backward hops, keeping the left leg straight and the upper body leaning out passively to the rear. Initially you should practise this without the shot.

Try to achieve a low, slow hop, keeping your shoulders square to the rear and turning your feet to the open side. It is essential that the right foot is the dominant propelling agent of the glide and that the

Fig 17 Gliding.

balanced chin–knee–toe position is adopted after the glide phase.

ADVANCED TECHNIQUE

Top-class shot putters use relaxed, efficient and rangy techniques when throwing long distances. The novice thrower should always remember that these techniques require great strength and power as well as skill. Never blindly copy the champions' techniques but adapt them to suit your own strength levels and physique.

Linear Technique

The Glide (Figs 18 to 21)

Adopt a relaxed posture at the rear of the circle; how low this position is will depend upon your strength as an athlete. Young athletes will start much higher than more experienced athletes. The glide begins with an off-balancing of the hips towards the centre of the circle, quickly followed by an extension of the rear leg and a 'stabbing' of the front leg towards the stop board. Leave the rear half of the circle heel first, shoulders square to the rear, left arm passive and relaxed. It helps to look back at an object a metre or two to the rear of the circle at this point; this avoids turning the head and shoulders prematurely during the glide. The right foot is pulled under the body ready to assume the power position.

Power Position (Figs 22 & 23)

The rear foot has grounded and has been turned inwards along with the right knee and hip. This gives a torque position – the displacement of the planes of upper and lower body – and aids a quick, whiplash

putting movement. If the rear foot is left pointing to the rear of the circle, there will be a delay in the movement at the centre of the circle. Adopt a chin–knee–toe position; if you are very strong, the plane of the chin–knee–toe position will be angled towards the rear. A young thrower will exhibit a vertical chin–knee–toe.

The shoulders and left arm have been held square to the rear and this is helped by the position of the head which still faces the rear of the circle. The feet are almost in line, with the front foot a little to the left of the putting direction. This allows the hips to be pushed through later in the put.

The Putting Action (Figs 24 to 29)

The final throw begins with the right hip being pushed forwards with a fast drive from the right leg. At this point you must keep the shot held back and allow your hips to lead the movement. Your weight should be pushed over your left leg with your hips assuming a position square to the direction of the throw. The left side of your body must be braced; straighten it as the putting arm strikes. It is essential that the arm strikes 'fast and last', with the elbow held high behind the shot. Look at the shot as it leaves your hand. The dynamic movement of your right leg and hip will cause your centre of gravity to push forward beyond your front foot and you may lose your balance. To recover from this, change feet and lower your centre of gravity; a good put can be saved by this simple manoeuvre at the very end of the throw.

This sequence does not convey the flow of movement from slow to fast. Try to concentrate on achieving a slow glide – feel the power position for a split second – and then exploding the shot away from the circle.

Fig 18 Mike Winch, Commonwealth Games medallist, shows a relaxed low posture at the start of the put.

Fig 19 The movement starts with an off-balancing of the hips.

Fig 20 The rear leg is fully extended.

Fig 21 The glide is low and fast.

Fig 22 The power position with hips open and shoulders closed.

Fig 23 The chin–knee–toe alignment.

Fig 24   The right hip pushes horizontally to the front.

Fig 25   The shot is held back.

Fig 26   The weight is pushed over the front foot.

Fig 27   With the hips square to the front, the putting arm strikes.

Fig 28   The arm punches the shot away.

Fig 29   Having used every centimetre of the circle, the athlete fights to save the throw.

Rotational Technique

An increasing number of shot putters are beginning to use a discus spin. It is advisable that all shot putters learn to throw from a spin as well as a glide, since they may ultimately throw further by using this technique.

The Turn (Figs 30 & 31)

Assume a comfortable sitting position at the back of the circle, holding the putting arm high at this point and throughout the throw. Transfer your weight from right to left, rotating around your left foot until you face the direction of the throw. Step down into the front half of the circle, keeping your throwing arm high. Your left foot must be quickly grounded at the front of the circle in line with the rear foot. Here, your weight must be allowed to drift between your feet while you keep your shoulders closed and hips open to the side.

The Throw (Fig 32)

There is a marked difference between the throwing action of the linear technique and that of the rotational technique. In the linear technique you pushed your hips to the front in a horizontal movement; in the rotational style the action is a two-legged lift upwards with only a slight horizontal movement of the hips. It is essential that the left side is blocked so that rotational velocity is transferred to linear velocity. The putting movement should be that of a two-legged lifting action.

(a)   (b)   (c)

*Fig 30   (a) Brian Oldfield (USA), former unofficial world record holder, 'sits' at
the rear of the circle. (b) Transferring the bodyweight from right foot to left.
(c) A balanced entry into the turn with the putting arm held high.*

Fig 31   (d) The athlete steps down into the front of the circle. (e) The left foot must be quickly grounded. (f) The power position.

Fig 32   (g) The beginning of an explosive, two-legged vertical lift. (h) The arm strikes 'fast and last'. (i) The feet are reversed to save the throw.

SHOT DRILLS

Linear

Fixed Feet (Fig 33)

By keeping both feet fixed to the ground throughout the throw, you can ensure that both legs are working to their utmost during the throw. Even throwers who throw with an active reverse find it beneficial to practise fixed feet throwing. Fixed feet can be practised both in a standing position and in a full put.

Fig 33   *Fixed feet throwing.*

Partial Puts

A difficult part of the technique to develop is the timing of the left leg and putting arm strike. By adopting a partial standing throw position you can concentrate on this last part of the total throwing action. This drill is also useful to develop a high, blocking left side.

Stop-check

In this drill you should freeze at the end of the glide. The frozen position can be checked for its effectiveness. After repositioning, the throw is completed by performing a standing throw.

Rotational

Half Turn (Fig 34)

The starting position is with the right foot in the centre of the circle and the left foot about 80cm to the rear. You should be wound up, and then push vigorously off the left leg. This initiates a fast right foot pivot so that the left foot is out of contact with the ground for as short a time as possible. From the middle position, the left foot grounds at the front of the circle and you should then perform the lifting, blocking movement.

One and a Half Turn (Fig 35)

Start with your left foot at the back of the circle, as for a normal turn, but facing the direction of the throw. Your right foot should be outside the circle, as far from the left foot as is comfortable and you should be in a wound up position. Start the movement by shifting your weight over your left leg and then driving (running) across the circle. You will arrive in the power position and should then complete the throw.

FAULTS AND CORRECTIONS

Fault   Too high in the middle of the circle (power position).
Cause   Glide from the back of the circle

The Shot

Fig 34   The half turn.

Fig 35   The one and a half turn.

was made without the upper body being passive and/or the starting position was too low for your strength.

Correction Alter starting position – practise low hops with your torso passive and held at 45 degrees to the ground.

Fault Leaving the rear leg behind during the glide phase and therefore being in an inefficient power position.

Cause Not pulling the rear foot under the body, and the friction caused by scraping the rear foot along the ground.

Correction Practise a low hop rather than gliding the foot over the ground. This will give a little extra time to pull the foot under the body. Practise a hop–stop–check power position throw drill.

Fault Shoulders not arriving in a closed position after the glide, lessening the range of movement.

Cause Shoulders and left arm are not passive during the glide phase.

Correction Practise repetition hops, keeping your left shoulder and left arm passive and relaxed. Look over your left wrist during the glide or try turning your left palm outwards. This creates tension in the straight left arm during the glide.

Fault Collapsing the left side (non-throwing side) of the body during the throw.

Cause Not bracing the left side during the throwing action.

Correction Go back to practising partial standing throws and fixed feet standing throws. Concentrate on finishing 'tall'.

Fault 'Bucketing' the left foot too far left of centre at the front of the circle. This will cause you to fall off to the left during the final throwing action.

Cause Opening the hips out too soon at the start of the glide.

Correction Keep the hips square to the back of the circle for the first part of the glide. Concentrate on stabbing the left foot down to the stop board during the glide phase.

Fault Reversing too early and putting without contact with the ground.

Cause Not transferring the weight from the rear to the front leg before the arm strike begins.

Correction Plenty of fixed feet drills, graduating to late reverse well after the shot has left the hand. In the power position, think of the rear leg action as initially driving the hip horizontally, transferring the weight over the front leg.

Fault Shot lands outside the sector to the right.

Cause Either blocking with the left foot and stopping the hips driving to the front, or rushing the movement and striking with the arm too early.

Correction Ensure that your left foot is aligned correctly in the power position. 'Feel' the power position before throwing and leave the arm 'fast and last'.

3 The Discus

Discus throwing is an event which requires time and repeated practice. Very few beginners can throw a really long way on their first efforts since the rotational technique requires rhythm and timing which develop gradually. For this reason discus throwers improve year after year, the classic example being Al Oerter, the four-time Olympic winner who threw his best distances in his mid-forties, twelve years after his last gold medal performance.

Physically the coach should look for athletes with long armed, rangy builds who, like all throwers, have the ability to make explosive, dynamic movements.

RULES (Fig 36)

The discus is thrown from a 2·50m circle into a 40 degree sector. The athlete must start from a stationary position and, after completing the throw, leave from the rear half of the circle. Unlike the shot and javelin events, no restrictions are placed on the method of throwing. Measurement of the throw is between the mark made by the discus closest to the circle, and the inside rim of the circle.

	Men	Women
Colt* (U–13)	1kg	0·75kg
Junior (U–15)	1·25kg	1kg
Intermediate		
(U–17)	1·5kg	1kg
Euro-Junior	(U–20)	(U–19)
	1·75kg	1kg
Senior	2kg	1kg
*recommended		

Fig 37   The competitive weights for discus throwing.

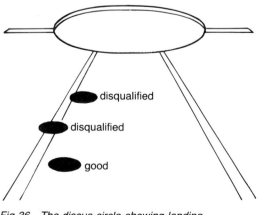

Fig 36   The discus circle showing landing positions for good and disqualified throws.

LEARNING TO THROW

The majority of novice athletes who fail to throw the discus well do so because they lack confidence in holding the discus. It is therefore essential that confidence is gained in handling the implement with the correct grip.

The Hold (Fig 38)

Place your throwing hand over the top of the discus with the fingers evenly spread. The discus should rest on the first joint of your fingers. It should not be gripped, but allowed to rest lightly on the first joints with the tips of your fingers curling over the rim. You should then test your grip by swinging the discus. Place it on your left hand at shoulder height in the same manner as a golf tee supports a golf ball. Then grip the discus with your right hand; swing it off the left hand, horizontally, to your right side and quickly back to your left hand.

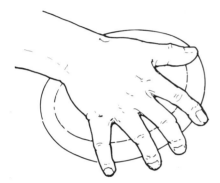

Fig 38   *The correct discus grip.*

Basic Throw

You can test this grip in the simplest form of throw. With feet facing the direction of the throw, take the discus from the left hand,

Fig 39   *Releasing the discus correctly from the index finger.*

swing it back across the body and then release it forwards. When you can release it confidently in this manner, you can move on to the standing throw.

Standing Throw (*Fig 40*)

The standing throw is the basic technical model for the event and accounts for over 80 per cent of the distance thrown. Assume a position, as in *Fig 40*, ensuring that chin, knee and toe are in vertical alignment and that your feet are 90cm apart. From this initial stance, withdraw the discus to a position behind your right shoulder, keeping your arm long and relaxed. This movement must be performed quickly to avoid the discus dropping from your hand.

From this position, perform a slinging motion initiated by your right hip driving to the front slightly ahead of your shoulders and arm. The arm must be kept relaxed and long with the hand flat and parallel to the ground (palm down). The throw is made around an erect, static left side of the body and it is helpful if the feet are kept fixed to the ground to give balance and stability. After a few initial throws, make sure the discus leaves the hand from the first finger and is released spinning in a clockwise direction. It is a mistake to release from the little finger.

Throwing with a Turn
(*Fig 41*)

Once the standing throw has been mastered and the discus is spinning out to reasonable distances, you should add a simple turn to the standing throw.

Assume a position at the back of the circle, standing sideways to the direction of the throw, and perform one or two preliminary swings. At the end of the back swing,

The Discus

Fig 40   The standing throw.

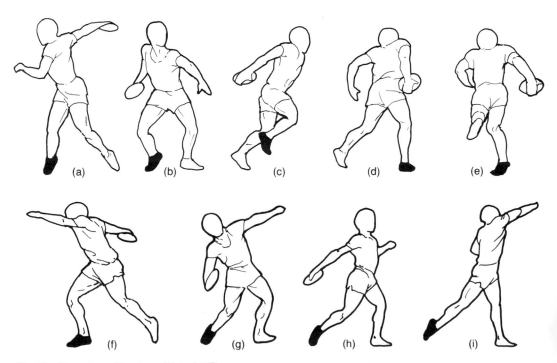

Fig 41   Throwing with a turn. (a) to (e) The
turn. (f) to (i) The power position to
the release.

step into the centre with the right foot and quickly ground the left foot at the front of the circle slightly off centre. Make this movement as simple as possible; think of it as a simple stepping motion along a straight line (which can be drawn, for guidance). This stepping action should bring you into the aligned chin–knee–toe position and again your hips should provide most of the power for the final slinging action. Aim to make this turning and stepping motion as balanced as possible; it will help if you keep your shoulders level throughout the turn and your eyes looking to the front, focused on an object on the horizon directly in front of the circle. Practise this as many times as possible to perfect a smooth, relaxed technique.

ADVANCED TECHNIQUE

Preliminary Swings (Fig 42)

Before assuming the position illustrated, you will have made two or three preliminary swings back and forth across your body to generate movement in the discus and rhythm in your body. During the swings you should transfer your weight from left to right but it is advisable to keep your right foot grounded on the backswing. These initial swings should not be fast but smooth, comfortable and made with a long, relaxed arm.

Entry to the Turn (Figs 43 to 45)

This is a critical moment in the throw since a small mistake here will be magnified by the time you complete the throw. You must transfer your weight from your right side to a position of balance over your left foot. On entry you should think of chin–knee–toe

being in vertical alignment. Assume a high sitting posture throughout this entry phase and lead the discus into the entry by the hips and legs. Your throwing arm should be long and relaxed and no effort should be made to force it back.

The Turn (Figs 46 & 47)

Rather than turning, you should think of running or sprinting across the circle, ahead of a trailing discus. At the end of your entry you should be facing the direction of the throw, slightly leaning into the centre of the circle, with your eyes fixed on an object on the horizon somewhere between the left sector line and the centre of the throwing sector. This focal point will help you to balance and achieve a linear drive across the circle. The turn is completed by a combination of a linear drive with the left leg (push) and a controlled swing of the right leg. The torso should be held erect throughout the movement and the left arm should reach for the centre of the circle and remain there, causing the body to wind up. It is important that you keep your right foot turning once it has been placed in the centre of the circle; this will help to keep you moving through the power position.

Power Position (Fig 48)

This is a key position which dictates just how far the discus will be thrown. The power position should exhibit two essential features – balance and range. Once again you should have chin–knee–toe in vertical alignment and be balanced over your rear leg, ready to throw. This balanced position is not a static one and should be passed through rather than posed. You will achieve superb range by allowing the hip axis to lead the shoulder axis, which in turn leads

Fig 42 Wolfgang Schmidt (GDR), former world record holder and Olympic medallist, at the end of his last preliminary swing.

Fig 43 The athlete 'sits' and transfers his weight from right to left.

Fig 44 It is essential that the athlete is balanced at the rear of the circle.

Fig 45 The eyes are fixed on the horizon and the discus trails behind the athlete.

Fig 46   The drive across the circle.

Fig 47   A long discus arm and quick feet.

Fig 48   The power position – balanced and
         rangy.

Fig 49   The right hip is pushed to the front,
         ahead of the discus.

Fig 50 The non-throwing side is braced.

Fig 51 The throwing arm comes in 'fast and last'.

Fig 52 The athlete 'chases' the discus out of the circle.

Fig 53 The feet are reversed to save the throw.

the discus. From this position great force can be applied over the range of movement, guaranteeing a high release speed. Good range is achieved by a sound entry position and quick feet – the right and left feet should be grounded very quickly ahead of the discus. If the left foot is slow to ground, range will be lost. You should aim for a fast, low, linear path of the left foot to the front of the circle. Your left foot should land slightly to the left of an imaginary centre line; this positioning will help your hips to come through to the front during the throw. If your left foot grounds to the right of the centre line (blocked), this hinders the free movement of the hip drive to the front.

The Throw (*Figs 49 to 51*)

The action of the throw is dominated by the action of the right leg which initiates the throwing movement. The throw is basically an explosive thrust of the right hip to the front, working against a braced left side whilst keeping the throwing arm long. The left arm, which has been long during the turn, is now shortened by flexing the elbow to 90 degrees and aids the drive to the front. The whole of the left side should block and allow the right side of the body to accelerate around it.

The throwing arm must not be allowed to drop down but must be kept at a 90 degree angle to the torso. The release must be over a tall left side, with the left foot in contact with the circle and a long, very fast arm coming through when all the other muscle groups have finished their work.

Recovery (*Figs 52 & 53*)

Provided you have mastered an effective left side block, staying within the confines of the circle should not be a problem. Your

feet should be reversed at the front of the circle and your centre of gravity lowered. The recovery (or reverse) must not take place prematurely, but immediately after the discus has left your hand. You should ensure that during training you throw within the confines of the 2·50m circle.

DISCUS DRILLS

Half Turn (*Fig 54*)

Whilst the standing throw is a valuable basic drill, it often lacks relevance to the total throw because it starts from a static position. In the full throw, the power position is merely passed through and not held statically. The half turn drill will enable you to simulate this moving power position from a simple turn.

Start the drill standing sideways to the direction of the throw, with your right foot on the centre line and left foot a little way from the back of the circle. Your weight should be mostly over your left leg and the discus in a fully wound position. Drive off your left foot and turn on your right foot into the standing throw position, completing the throw without stopping.

Run Across (*Fig 55*)

This drill is used to give linear drive to the throw and can be used by novice or advanced throwers. Assume a position at the back of the circle, standing sideways to the direction of the throw, with your left foot just inside the circle, pointing to the front, and your right foot 50cm to the rear of the circle. You are now in a wound-up position with the balance over your front foot. Drive across the circle into the power position and complete the throw.

The Discus

Fig 54   The half turn.

Fig 55   The run across.

FAULTS AND CORRECTIONS

Fault   Off balance during the throw.
Cause   Usually this can be traced to the rear of the circle and failing to enter on balance. Poor head alignment can also cause imbalance.
Correction   Ensure that a balanced chin–knee–toe position is assumed at the rear of the circle. Use a focal point to keep the head stable and aligned.

Fault   Not using the whole of the circle and falling off the throw, particularly to the left and rear.
Cause   Not driving across the circle during the turn and turning too early off the back of the circle.
Correction   On entry, look at your focal point and run across the circle when your chest is in the direction of the throw. The South African (one and a half turn) drill can be used to establish linear drive across the circle.

Fault   Falling off to the left during the final throwing action.
Cause   Either the left foot is 'bucketed' (too far to the left) or the non-throwing side is not blocked.
Correction   Ensure that the left foot pushes off the back of the circle and takes a quick linear path to the front of the circle. Check feet alignment. Emphasise left arm – left side block during fixed feet drills both from standing and full throws.

Fault   You stop in the middle of the circle.
Cause   Lack of strength or your right foot lands flat and static in the centre of the circle.
Correction   Check whether your power position is too deep or rangy for your strength. Ensure that you are landing on the ball of your right foot and that it keeps turning.

Fault   Lack of range in the throw.
Cause   Landing with the shoulders in an open position in the power position. The discus is not far enough to the rear of the right hip when the power position is reached.
Correction   Ensure that the left arm does not pull away too soon and that it continues to reach out to the back of the circle. The power position should be reached by quick feet; this keeps the hips ahead of the shoulders and the throwing arm.

Fault   Discus stalling and not spinning.
Cause   Being back off the throw (not following it out) at the moment of release and possibly having an incorrect grip.
Correction   Keep your palm down and hand flat during release. Concentrate on driving the discus out horizontally. Check your grip. If it is correct, try an alternative grip with your first two fingers together. Be aware of pressing down on the discus with your thumb during the final arm action.

4 The Hammer

The hammer is a much neglected event in schools and clubs. It is perceived as a dangerous and complicated event; this is an incorrect judgement if common sense is applied. It is certainly a rewarding event for any athlete since the heavy implement travels a long way from the circle.

Hammer throwing depends less on natural ability and more on hard work and training. The layman's idea that a large, rotund person will automatically excel at hammer is incorrect; we are in fact looking for an athletic, explosive thrower with superb technique. An athlete of average size can compete with distinction in the hammer event if he is prepared to take time to master the skills.

RULES *(Fig 57)*

The hammer is thrown from a circle 2·13m in diameter but, unlike in the shot, there is no stop board. The implement, once thrown, has to land within a 40 degree sector. No restriction is placed upon the style of throw but, as in the shot and discus, the start must be stationary and the thrower must leave by the rear half of the circle in a controlled manner and after the implement has landed.

The hammer consists of a metal ball with a length of wire and a stirrup type grip connected to it by a swivel attachment. The overall length of the implement is approximately four feet.

	Men
Colt* (U–13)	3·25kg
Junior (U–15)	4kg
Intermediate (U–17)	5kg
Euro-Junior (U–20)	6·25kg
Senior	7·26kg
*recommended	

Fig 56   The competitive weights for hammer throwing.

There are no official recommended weights for women and up to the 1980s this event was restricted to men. Recently, however, informal women's competitions have been

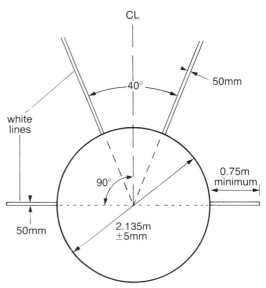

Fig 57   The dimensions of the hammer circle.

taking place and it is likely that official competitions and championships will soon become established within the sport.

LEARNING TO THROW

The Hold (*Fig 58*)

The hammer handle is held in the left hand so that the grip lies along the base of the fingers. Grip with the right hand in a similar way so that the fingers overlap those of the left hand. Novices will find little need to wear a protective glove but as distances increase to over 30 metres, the friction caused by the handle on release will necessitate the wearing of a strong leather glove on the left hand.

Fig 58   The correctly gripped hammer.

Swings (*Fig 59*)

The swings are used to give the hammer initial speed and rhythm. Start with the hammer placed to your right and behind your feet. From this position, pull the hammer across your body, keeping your arms straight in front of your body and bending them to catch the hammer behind your head. Skilful throwers can relax their arms and power the swings by moving their hips counter to the hammer; for example, when the hammer is to the right of the body, the hips counter to the left. As the speed of the swings increases, bend your legs to maintain balance. Although the hammer will start to your right, during the swings its low point will move progressively round to establish itself just off your right foot. The high point, of course, will then be directly behind your left shoulder.

Basic Throw

You should perform three swings, smoothly increasing your speed, and then release the hammer over your left shoulder, slightly turning into the throw and standing tall and solid. Satisfactory distances can be achieved by this method.

The Turns (*Fig 60*)

Without the Hammer

World-class throwers use either three or four turns to accelerate the hammer and even if you are a novice, you should attempt to turn as soon as possible. It is best to learn the technique of the 'heel and ball' turn by performing it initially without the hammer.

Shift your weight slightly over your left foot and start the movement by turning both

The Hammer

Fig 59   Swinging the hammer.

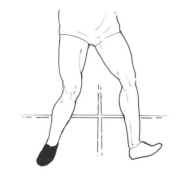

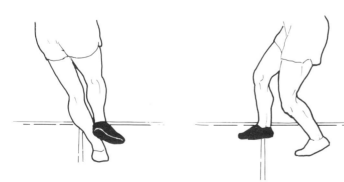

Fig 60   Practise footwork for the turns
without the hammer.

feet simultaneously; the toe of the left foot should be picked up and turned to the front of the circle and the heel of the right foot turned. You will need to turn the left toe a full 180 degrees before transferring your weight on to it. Complete the turn by picking up the right knee quickly and replacing it parallel to the left foot. Keep both legs bent and your back straight, arms passive and head erect – don't look down at your feet! After your first attempts, it is helpful to hold a football at arm's length to simulate the holding of the hammer.

With the Hammer

Once you are competent at turning without the hammer, you should try to add two turns on to your swings. Remember to keep your weight over your left leg on entry, arms straight, legs bent, eyes looking at the hammer head. Once the transition has been made from swings to the turns, your arms should be kept long and straight and you should feel the pull at the shoulders. You will be eager to throw for distance but at first you should perform multiple turns without releasing the hammer in order to perfect your turning skill.

Short Hammer Method
(*Fig 61*)

Youngsters often find turning with a four foot long hammer difficult and frustrating because the pull of a long hammer affects balance. As an alternative, a short hammer can be used when developing the turns.

A short hammer is improvised by removing the hammer wire and replacing it either with two interlocking 'D' shackles or with a short piece of nylon cord, of more than 230kg breaking strain, tied in a knot which will not slip, such as a bowline.

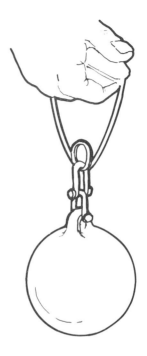

Fig 61   The short hammer.

Standing Throw (*Figs 62 & 63*)

With the short hammer at your right knee, throw the implement over your left shoulder using your legs and arms to lift. You should turn sideways and finish stretched high on your toes.

Next, move on to perform a pendulum swing, starting with the hammer at your left side, swung forward to the centre, back to your right side, then delivered over your left shoulder. From this 'V' swing, you can enter and perform your turns before releasing. Gradually increase the length of hammer as you master the skill of turning until you are able to use the four foot hammer.

Fig 62 *Starting the standing throw with the short hammer at the right knee.*

ADVANCED TECHNIQUE

Preliminary Swings
(*Figs 65 to 69*)

You must ensure that the preliminary swings are correctly performed as the balance, rhythm, and plane of the hammer are all established by well-performed swings. Adopt a shoulder width leg stance at the rear of the circle. The hammer can be started by either of two methods: the static method where the hammer is positioned on the ground to your right at the rear and is then swung across your body; or by a pendulum swing, where the hammer starts to your rear at the left and is swung first forward to the centre and then to the right

Fig 63 *Completing the standing throw stretched high on the toes.*

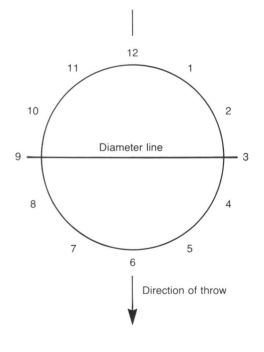

Fig 64 *The 'clock' orientation of the hammer circle.*

rear. This latter method, when perfected, gives a little more rhythm and makes the first swing much easier to perform.

Matthias Moder has completed his first swing and starts his second swing. Top-class performers usually perform two swings before entering into the turn phase. The second swing is always faster than the first. The hammer is approaching the low point which will be just off the right foot (between 1 and 2 o'clock). The arms are long and relaxed, legs slightly flexed. The hips look centred but are moving across to counter the pull of the hammer. The counter of the hips and the flexing of the knees enable the athlete to oppose the position of the hammer with his body throughout the swings. As the hammer approaches its high point, the hips have moved to the thrower's right to counter the pull of the implement. As the hammer passes in front of the athlete, the arms are long, but as it passes behind the head, the arms are quickly bent and the torso turns to catch the hammer at the very end of the swing. Only the shoulders turn; the head, hips, knees and feet remain facing the rear of the circle.

Entry *(Figs 69 & 70)*

This is a crucial stage of the throw where success or failure is determined since the balance of the turns is decided here. At the end of the last swing, just before the low point is reached, your hips and weight should be moved slightly over the left heel. Your arms should be kept low, knees flexed and hands low. As the hammer passes your right foot, press your right hip into the turn; and foot, knee and hip should all turn with the hammer. Both feet turn anti-clockwise with the hammer itself. The entry phase is a long one, with the right foot not breaking contact with the ground until it has reached 9 or 10 o'clock. You will have formed an isosceles triangle with your shoulders and arms, providing the longest possible radius for your turns, especially if your shoulders are relaxed. Push the hammer out to the left on entry. It is important that you fix your eyes on either the hammer head or on a point just beyond the hammer. This entry should not be rushed, so concentrate on keeping it the same speed as the second swing, certainly no faster.

First Turns *(Figs 71 to 73)*

The athlete in this sequence is a four turn thrower. Indeed, the majority of world-class throwers use four turns but three turns are potentially as good and should not be thought of as inferior. When using four turns, it is necessary to perform the first turn on the left toe; do not use the conventional heel and ball turn. Turns two, three and four will be performed using the heel and ball method. The toe turn is more difficult to perform and time must be spent perfecting its balance. There is a total transfer of weight on to the left toe as the high point is reached. At the high point, try to keep your radius long. The right foot, which comes off at 9 o'clock, makes a close, quick step over, to land facing the hammer. This is an essential part of modern hammer throwing – you must stay *on* the hammer, not lead it. At the completion of the turn, the hips and knees should be on, or only fractionally ahead of, the implement.

From this position, you should feel the acceleration of the hammer. Early left heel contact is vital, as is the continuous turning of both knees. Sit in the double support phases; however, the depth illustrated here is exceptional and should not be copied by the inexperienced.

Fig 65　Matthias Moder (GDR) at the
　　　　beginning of his last swing.

Fig 66　His weight is transferred from right
　　　　to left.

Fig 67　The arms bend as the hammer
　　　　travels behind the athlete.

Fig 68　The torso turns to catch the
　　　　hammer.

Fig 69 The beginning of the entry – arms long and low.

Fig 70 A balanced entry.

Fig 71 The first turn – arms long and fast feet.

Fig 72 The right foot must keep with the hammer.

Fig 73 The end of the first turn – the hips face the hammer.

Fig 74 The start of the second turn.

Fig 75 Midway through the second turn.

Fig 76 The end of the second turn – the athlete 'sits' to counter the strong pull of the hammer.

Fig 77   The start of the third turn.

Fig 78   The plane of the hammer steepens.

Fig 79   End of the third turn.

Fig 80   The fourth turn.

Fig 81 The athlete counters the pull of the hammer.

Fig 82 The delivery – the athlete keeps his arms long and turns his legs and torso to the front.

Fig 83 The legs are explosively straightened.

Fig 84 The hammer is released at full stretch.

Turns Two to Four
(*Figs 74 to 81*)

The speed of the hammer increases with each turn and the technical points to be emphasised are:

1. Keep the shoulders relaxed and the arms long.
2. Let the hammer out at the high point.
3. Keep the left leg bent throughout the turns.
4. The left foot should exhibit continuity in the turn.
5. There should be a vigorous pumping action of the right leg, which is kept tight into the left thigh.
6. Hips should be kept on the hammer throughout the turns.
7. The head is stable throughout, with the eyes looking at the hammer.

Fig 85 *Letting the hammer out at the high point while increasing the speed of the turns.*

8. Once the right foot has grounded, work both legs by twisting the knees around in the direction of the throw – be active.
9. Weight will transfer from right to left foot when the hammer is on the left, and back to the right foot on the end of the single support phase. This transfer is not total and requires only a slight shift of weight.
10. Catch the hammer early so that the double support phase is long. Let the hammer run its own course from 4 o'clock through to 9 o'clock.
11. Develop rhythm in the turns, letting the hammer create its own rhythm. The hammer will build its own acceleration, so do not accelerate too much yourself or try to lead it round.
12. Keep the torso erect throughout the throw.

The Delivery (*Figs 80 to 84*)

Start the delivery as soon as the right foot makes ground contact at the end of the fourth turn. The hammer should be caught high and to the right. Continue to turn your legs and torso at the high point, beating the hammer down to its low point with your legs remaining flexed. When the hammer reaches its low point, straighten your legs explosively and block your left side. The strong, vertical lift over a flat, solid left foot should be finished with a whip of the arms which have been kept long and straight throughout the movement.

DRILLS

Multiple Turning
(*Figs 86 & 87*)

The more turns you can perform, the more your skill improves. You should attempt to

The Hammer

Fig 86 It can be helpful to use a pole to simulate the hammer when practising turning drills.

Fig 87 Holding the pole across the shoulders in turning drills.

perform four to six turns, but without accelerating. Concentrate on the turning skill
without worrying about throwing a long
way. Turning drills without the hammer can
be most beneficial using a pole to simulate
the implement. Alternatively, the pole can
be held across the shoulders.

Swing and Turn Combinations

Start at the back of the circle by performing
two swings; enter and perform two controlled turns, followed by two swings, followed
by two turns. This drill, which has numerous
variations, will teach you control of the
hammer.

You will find it satisfying to throw the
hammer at the end of a set of multiple turns
and swings.

Short Hammer Deliveries

Using a shorter wire, concentrate on delivery technique using one or two turns. Three
or four turns can be used, taking the first
two or three turns easily and slowly and
finishing off with a fast last turn and delivery.

FAULTS AND CORRECTIONS

Fault   Lack of balance during turns.
Cause   Usually you will have been unba-
lanced when entering the first turn.
Correction   Practise swing and turn drills.
Ensure that you are balanced on entry.

Fault   Acceleration phase of the hammer
is too brief.
Cause   Squaring of the hips when the right
foot is grounded.
Correction   Practise turning with the hammer, keeping the hips on the hammer at the
moment of right foot contact.

Fault   Losing contact with the ground and
jump-turning.
Cause   Hammer plane is too steep and
you are unbalanced.
Correction   Do not let your hands go
above shoulder level; keep your legs bent
and active during the turns.

Fault   Poor delivery.
Cause   The low point of the hammer is too
far to your left at the end of the last turn. You
are unbalanced.
Correction   Ensure that the low point of the
hammer is correct at entry and that the right
foot is fast and active; use turning drills to
improve balance.

Fault   Turning with the arms bent.
Cause   Inability to withstand the pull of the
hammer, due to imbalance. The bending of
the arms reduces the pull.
Correction   Turning drills to ensure that
you are turning on bent knees and that you
push your hands away and keep elbows
close. You should feel the pull of the
hammer on your shoulders.

Fault   Pulling the head and left shoulder
away from the hammer.
Cause   Tension and trying too hard to
quicken and accelerate the hammer.
Correction   Look at the hammer head or
just in front of the hammer. Keep the
shoulders long and on the hammer.

5 The Javelin

Throwing the javelin is a popular event with youngsters. World-class javelin throwers are much lighter than other elite throwers, with physiques akin to decathletes and heptathletes because the event relies much more on speed and explosive power than on strength. Athletes of average physical build have proved successful and, indeed, have won medals and set records.

RULES (Fig 89)

The throw, unlike the other throwing events, is made from a runway which is between 30 and 36·5m long and 4m wide. The javelin is thrown into a 29 degrees arc. The throw, to be valid, must land point first but does not have to stick in to the ground or even make a mark. The rules specify the method of throwing which is over the shoulder and not hurled or thrown discus style.

	Men	Women
Colt* (U–13)	400g	400g
Junior (U–15)	600g	600g
Intermediate		
(U–17)	700g	600g
Euro-Junior	(U–20)	(U–19)
	800g	600g
Senior	800g	600g
*recommended		

Fig 88   Weights for competitive javelin throwing.

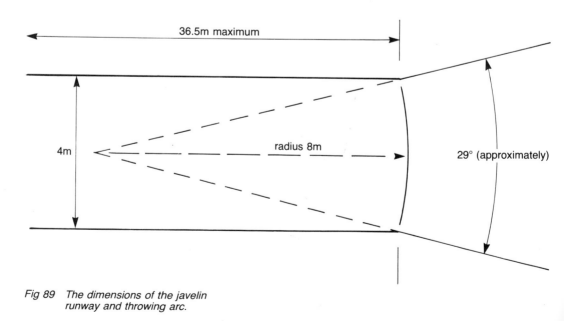

Fig 89   The dimensions of the javelin runway and throwing arc.

LEARNING TO THROW

Grip (*Fig 90*)

It is essential that a strong, stable grip is acquired. The grip must remain firm behind the ledge made by the binding (cord), and the javelin must run down the length of the palm and not across it. The fingers which are not secured behind the binding must press firmly on the javelin in order to produce a natural spin at release. There are three main grips to choose from.

The V grip is probably the easiest and surest method of gripping the javelin for novice throwers, although the second finger and thumb grip is the one most popular amongst experienced athletes. Whichever grip you prefer, it must be strong and stable with the wrist held tight.

Having chosen your grip, you must test its effectiveness by simply stabbing the javelin into the ground from a position above your head. If the binding has been held tight, the implement should stick into the ground.

The Standing Throw (*Fig 91*)

Adopt a stance with chin, knee and toe in alignment and the javelin held at full arm's length (but not a rigidly straight arm). Start the throw by driving your hips to the front ahead of your right shoulder. The arm strike is made once the shoulder is moving. Your elbow should be kept high and close to the javelin.

Three Stride Throw (*Fig 92*)

Face the direction of the throw with feet together and the javelin fully withdrawn, close to the arm. Your left foot should stride forward, followed by a longer, higher stride with the right foot; the sequence should be left – big stride – throw.

The emphasis of the big stride will leave your weight back over your rear right leg, giving a strong, rangy throwing position. The three strides should be made on flat feet, not on your toes. Again, the action of the right hip should be stressed.

When the three stride throw has been mastered, the run can be lengthened but always by two steps at a time; that is, it can be five, seven or nine. For the beginner, nine strides is the optimum approach pattern, although the average youngster is unlikely to progress beyond a simple five stride approach.

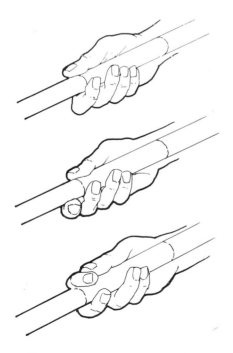

Fig 90 The correct javelin grip.

The Javelin

Fig 91   The standing throw.

Fig 92   The three stride throw.

ADVANCED TECHNIQUE

The technique used by the top-class per-
former consists of an approach run of
approximately thirty metres followed by the
throw. This approach is carefully phased to
produce optimum speed, range and
power.

1. Approach run (10 to 12 strides).
2. Withdrawal phase (2 strides).
3. Cross over (1 stride).
4. Throw (1 stride).
5. Recovery (1 stride).

These are not distinct, disjointed parts of
the throw but smooth, accelerating and co-
ordinated parts of the whole movement.

Approach (Fig 94)

This usually consists of between 10 and 12
strides and the objective is a smooth build-
up of speed to a point five strides from the

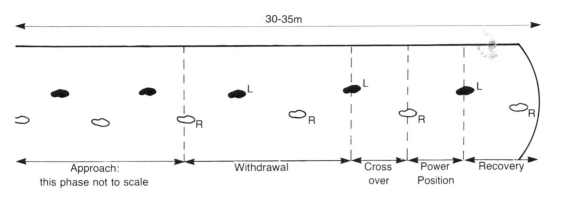

Fig 93 Footwork for an approach run of about 30m at advanced level.

scratch line. You must reach this point (between 9 and 12 metres away from the scratch line) balanced and at optimum speed. The javelin is carried above the shoulder, palm upwards, elbow under the javelin. You should be leaning forward slightly and should adopt a smooth, relaxed running motion. It is important that the javelin is held steady and flat.

Withdrawal Phase
(*Figs 95 to 99*)

From the running position the javelin must be withdrawn to its throwing position. This withdrawal usually takes two strides to accomplish and should not be rushed. When taken back, the javelin is aligned with the throwing angle; the throwing hand is kept high and rigid. The shoulders turn sideways to give the throw range but the hips and feet still point to the front so that running speed is maintained. This torque position requires mobility of both the shoulders and the hips.

Cross Over Strides
(*Figs 100 to 103*)

The stride immediately following the withdrawal regains the speed lost when the javelin is taken back. This stride, off the right leg, must be a driving stride. The javelin is kept back and aligned on a straight right arm.

The cross over stride follows. This pre-throwing stride is of crucial importance because it sets up the whole throw. Your left arm should be wrapped across your body and, together with a high chin, should give a torque throwing position. Your right knee should be picked up high at speed and your legs should move in front of your torso to allow you to lean back for greater range when the throw is made. Whilst your shoulders remain sideways, your hips and legs should still primarily face the direction of the throw.

Fig 94　David Ottley (GB), Olympic medallist, shows the javelin approach. The javelin is held steady and horizontal.

Fig 95　The withdrawal phase starts.

Fig 96　The approach speed must not decrease as the javelin is withdrawn.

Fig 97　The shoulders are now facing sideways to the direction of the throw.

Fig 98   The javelin is aligned with its throwing angle.

Fig 99   The hips should face the direction of the throw.

Fig 100   The pre-cross over stride is a driving stride.

Fig 101   The left arm must be kept wrapped across the body.

Fig 102 The right knee is picked up fast and high.

Fig 103 The legs lead the throwing arm into the power position.

Fig 104 The power position.

Fig 105 The drive of the right hip begins.

Fig 106 The hip drive continues.

Fig 107 The left foot is grounded and the 'bow' position shown.

Fig 108   The arm is used quickly with the
hand high and the javelin close to
the head.

Fig 109   The elbow leads the way.

Fig 110   The strong firm grip finishes the
throw.

Fig 111   The athlete follows through.

Fig 112   The eyes follow the flight of the
javelin.

Fig 113   The feet are reversed to save the
throw.

Power Position (*Fig 104*)

You should land on the flat of your right foot which points in the direction of your throw. If you find it difficult to achieve an extensive lean backwards, a lesser lean is acceptable. The javelin should be held back on a straight throwing arm, with your left arm still partially wrapped across your chest. The right foot is at approximately 30 degrees and ready to strike and the left leg is quickly moving through to ground. The javelin alignment should mirror the release angle. It is essential that the wrist position is kept firm so that the tip of the javelin is not raised too high.

Fig 114   The power position.

The Throw (*Figs 105 to 112*)

The action of the right hip and leg is the key feature of the throw. Before the left leg has grounded, the right heel whips around,

triggering off the explosive movement of the right hip to the front. Your chest is now fully to the front and your arm long and passive. Your left leg should have grounded quickly to provide a base and resistance for the right side of your body to act against. Only very powerful athletes have an extensive base and the ability to move over the front leg. Younger athletes should aim for a narrower base. Your arm is then used quickly with your hand remaining high and your elbow close to your head. Your non-throwing shoulder should be kept high, the left side of your body firm, and your left arm close to your side. It is important to keep your arm action 'fast and last' after your heel–leg–hip–trunk–shoulder movements have accelerated the implement.

Recovery (*Fig 113*)

Your front foot should be at least one body length away from the scratch line to prevent you from fouling the throw. Think of the recovery as a run through with your right leg which comes through to cushion forward momentum and not to reverse it, as in shot and discus. When your right foot lands, your knee should bend in order to lower your centre of gravity and prevent fouling. A good throw will always be difficult to save since the forward propulsion is considerable.

DRILLS

Running

For the novice the ability to run with the javelin in a relaxed manner is essential. Repeating runs of varying speeds will quickly develop a natural running action.

Withdrawal

During the actual throw, it is vital that when the implement is withdrawn, the overall speed is not radically reduced. Practise withdrawing the javelin and running ahead of it whilst keeping it fully withdrawn. The javelin alignment should always be checked.

Stop and Check

Perform a series of run-ups followed by the withdrawal. Stop in the pre-delivery stride to check javelin alignment, feet positioning and weight distribution.

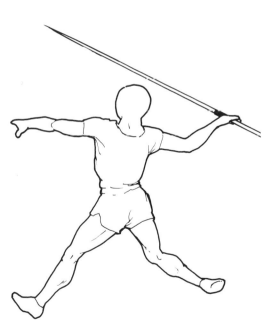

Fig 115   Stopping in the pre-delivery stride to check javelin alignment, feet positioning and weight distribution.

Restricted Approach

Far too often, novices throw continually from a full approach run and, because of the speed, cannot hope to develop an effective throwing action. A great deal of time should be spent on throwing from a three and five stride approach in order to concentrate on the pre-delivery stride and the final throwing action. At all times of the year, three and five stride work will have to form the bulk of your throwing session, except when you are specifically preparing for an important competition when the whole approach and throw must be perfected.

FAULTS AND CORRECTIONS

Fault   Throwing with the arm only and not with the legs.
Cause   Short base, poor power position.
Correction From a short approach, ensure that your base is adequately long, that your foot alignment is correct and your left foot is not blocking.

Fault   Javelin stalls and lands tail first.
Cause   Release angle incorrect. Not enough power in the throw.
Correction Ensure that your throwing hand is kept high and your wrist tight. Keep the tip of the javelin at head height before your arm strike.

Fault   Javelin lands too far to the left of the sector.
Cause   Not enough block on the left side.
Correction   Throw from a braced left side and do not make the recovery until the javelin is released.

The Javelin

Fault The javelin lands too far to the right side of the sector.

Cause 'Bucketing' the left leg too far to the left; javelin arm is too far to the right on release.

Correction Ensure that there is adequate block on the left side and that your feet are correctly aligned. Make sure that the javelin is released high and towards the centre.

Fault Excessive javelin vibration during flight.

Cause Incorrect application of power.

Correction Don't drag your arm down before release. Throw through the point of the javelin.

6 Fitness for Throwing

Without correct technique, long distances cannot be achieved. However, throwing is a combination of many physical components and *any* weaknesses will result in poor performances. Each physical component can be improved by training to enhance your overall fitness for throwing.

STRENGTH

Without strength you could not even pick up a shot, let alone throw it. To throw good distances, you must be able to handle the implements easily and to move them at great speed. This requires strength which is acquired over a number of years. The development of strength must be a gradual process, progressing from general simple exercises to a training regime which resembles that of an Olympic weightlifter.

The Novice

The young athlete has relatively soft bones and inadequate skeletal muscle. If you are a novice thrower, you should aim to build all-round strength without overloading your young physique. It is not necessary to use expensive equipment as, initially, exercises to build up your weight will develop the foundation of strength required. Some basic tried and tested exercises will provide suitable resistance for novices in all throwing events. The exercises in *Fig 116* are a few of the many exercises that can be used.

Making a Start (*Figs 117 to 119*)

In the first instance, you should perform several repetitions of each exercise (10 to 15) with light resistance. After this initial training, the repetitions should be lowered to 8 to 10 to develop strength rather than strength endurance. Performing simple exercises such as the basic press up you will quickly exceed the required 10 repetitions through a combination of increased strength and co-ordination.

Almost every exercise can be adapted to increase the overload: in the press up, by raising the feet and then performing it with a clap, the repetitions can be kept to the desired 8 to 10 while strength is developed.

Overloading

To overload the body it is better to perform multiple sets of exercises rather than a single set. Perform a first set of 10 repetitions, rest for 90 seconds, perform a second set of 10, rest for 90 seconds and perform a final set of 10 repetitions. This simple system is sound and useful for the novice. It is important to stimulate the muscles more than once a week. Three sessions, evenly spaced, each week are ideal but consecutive days must be avoided since the body needs to recover.

Not too much emphasis should be put on traditional methods of strengthening the leg muscles because these invariably involve loading the spine with weight across the shoulders and this can lead to injury in the young athlete.

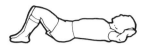

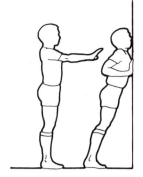

Crunchies

Push-offs

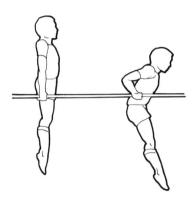

Wall bar knee raise

Dips

Leg curls

Fig 116 Basic bodyweight and medicine
ball strengthening exercises.

Vertical jumps

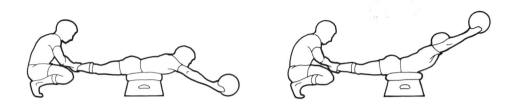

Back extensions

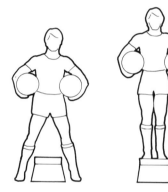

Astride jumps

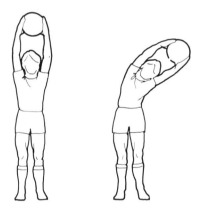

Side bends

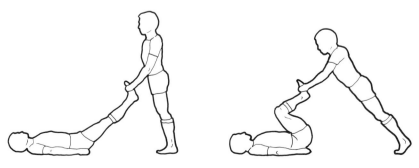

Partner-resisted leg press

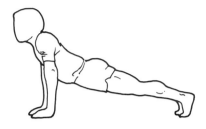
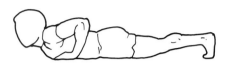

Fig 117   Press up.

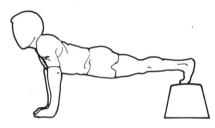
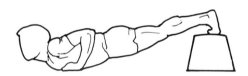

Fig 118   Decline press up.

Clap

Fig 119   Press up with a clap.

Intermediate

Having laid the foundations of all-round strength development, you are ready to move on to more advanced methods of strength training such as barbells and dumb-bells or using multi-gym weight-training apparatus.

A period of time should be spent on learning how to handle weight-lifting equipment and during this period the weights should be light, with many repetitions (between 10 and 15). It is essential that you are taught good technique and safety rules at an early stage. As in novice training, the aim is to produce all-round strength gains and not to specialise too early. Exercises to choose from are numerous but they must include at least one from each of the following groups:

Leg Exercises *(Figs 120 to 126)*

It is essential that strong legs are developed but care must be taken to build up this strength progressively. Early exercises should avoid overloading the spine by placing weights on the shoulders; exercises such as dumb-bell jump squats and leg presses should be used. Next, use the front squat, where the weight is held on the front of the shoulders. Eventually orthodox squats can be practised but care must be taken to ensure correct technique and safety.

Fig 121   Jump squat – start.

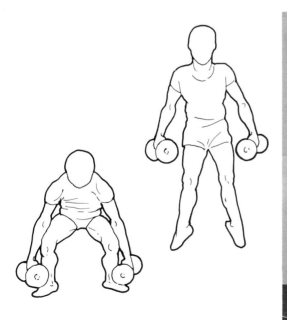

Fig 120   Jump squat.

Fig 122   Jump squat – finish.

Fig 123 Leg press.

Fig 124 Leg press – mid-point.

Fig 125 Front squat.

Fig 126 Orthodox squat.

Pulling (Figs 127 & 128)

The lifting of a barbell from the ground to the chest (clean) or above the head (snatch) is excellent for developing the lower back and leg strength. In addition to this, pulling develops the co-ordination of back and legs in a similar movement pattern to that of throwing (the summation of the body's forces). There are innumerable variations based on 'snatching' and 'cleaning'.

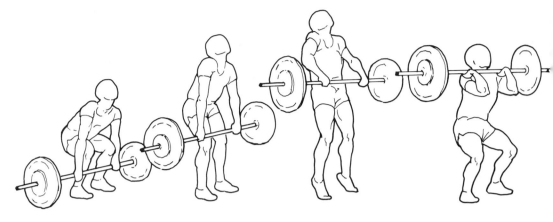

Fig 127   Power clean.

Fig 128   Power snatch.

Pressing (Figs 129 & 130)

This is probably the least important exercise to the thrower, when compared with those previously mentioned, but it is far too often given most priority by athletes. Exercises such as the bench press and simple press are standard, although there are many variations. Care must be taken when lifting above the head since back injuries can result if the torso has not previously been strengthened.

Fig 129 Bench press.

Fig 130 Press.

Fitness for Throwing

Torso

This area is far too often neglected by the thrower simply because strengthening the torso does not result in large weights being lifted which can be boasted about to friends and competitors. However, this area is of vital importance because it provides the link between leg strength and upper body strength. So much of throwing depends upon rotation; the muscles of the back and stomach provide much of that rotation as well as protecting the spine from injury. There are many exercises to choose from including sit-ups, side bends and hyper-extensions.

Fig 131   Sit-up.

Fig 132   Hyper-extensions.

Fig 133   Side bends.

Specific Exercises

At intermediate level you should also include some exercises specific to your event:

Shot – incline press
Discus – bent arm flies
Hammer – disc rotations
Javelin – French press and bent arm pullover

Fig 134   Incline press.

Fig 135   Start and finish point and mid point of bent arm flies.

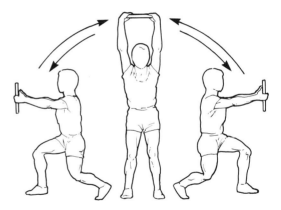

Fig 136   Disc rotations.

Fig 137   French press.

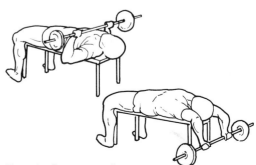

Fig 138   Bent arm pullovers.

Scheduling

You must train consistently on a progressive schedule. It is important to make constant changes to your routine to avoid boredom, which results if you keep to the same schedule for a whole year. A schedule might look like this:

September and October (4 weeks)

As many exercises as possible following a system of 3 sets of 10 repetitions with a short recovery (90 seconds) between each set and each exercise. The aim here is to condition the whole muscular system in three training sessions a week.

October, November and December (8 weeks)

Maintaining three sessions a week, reduce the number of exercises.

1. Squat: 2 warm-up sets followed by 10–8–6 repetitions, with the weight increased on each set. Squat only twice each week.
2. Bench press: 2 warm-up sets followed by 12–8–6–6 repetitions.
3. Clean: 2 warm-up sets followed by 10–8–6–4 repetitions.
4. Press: 2 warm-up sets followed by 8–8–8 repetitions.
5. Sit-ups: 3 sets of 20; side bends 3 sets of 10.

Late December (2 weeks)

An easy two week period playing with weights and moderate poundages.

January and February (8 weeks)

The intensity is increased, as is the volume.

1. Squat: 10–6–4–4
2. Bench press: 10–8–6–4–4
3. Clean: 8–6–4–2
4. Press: 6–6–6–6
5. Specialist exercises, for example French press for javelin: 3 sets of 10.
6. Sit-ups: 3 sets of 15
7. Side bends: 3 sets of 8

All exercises to have 2 to 3 sets as a warm-up: only squat once a week.

March and April

Continue as before but vary the exercises: front squat for squat, incline bench for bench press, snatch for clean, press behind neck for press.

May Onwards

In the competitive season it would be a mistake to continue to try and gain strength; lifting heavy weights takes up a great deal of energy and at this time of year technique and sharpness would suffer. Do not stop weight-training completely, since strength gained through the long winter months would gradually be lost, but aim to maintain rather than to increase strength. One or two strength sessions each week (at most) should be enough. The weight of the barbell should be reduced by 10 or 20 per cent to enable you to snap out the repetitions explosively. The total volume should also be reduced from 6 to 7 sets per exercise to 4 to 5 sets.

Advanced Schedules

As the athlete becomes more experienced, the overload must become greater, with heavier weights, more sets and more exercises performed. It is also necessary to introduce more variation; do not keep the overload constant. A six week strength block could take on the following loading changes.

	Session 1	Session 2	Session 3
Week 1	A (80% of max)	B (87½% of max)	C (92½% of max)
Week 2	C (92½%)	A (80%)	B (90%)
Week 3	A (82½%)	A (82½%)	C (95%)
Week 4	B (90%)	A (82½%)	C (95%)
Week 5	A (85%)	A (85%)	B (92½%)
Week 6	A (85%)	B (90%)	C (97½%)

Session A – 8 repetitions
Session B – 5 repetitions
Session C – 3 repetitions

In the six week block above the loading is changed progressively and a five per cent strength increase is achieved.

It is impossible to increase your strength week after week and you should be content with about three strength gain blocks each year, alternated with weeks of strength training of lesser volume and intensity.

Preparing for Competition

Having gained a significant amount of strength during the winter, you may be faced with the problem of converting this weight-lifting strength to throwing strength, often poles apart. Gradually quickening the execution of your lifts will help and, as the season approaches, the weights should be handled explosively. Sprinting, bounding, jumping and throwing will all help to gain the quickness so essential for throwing long distances.

Success has also been achieved by combining stretch reflex exercises with conventional weight-lifting exercises. This is most useful in the run up to a competition where conventional weight exercises are immediately followed by stretch reflex exercises involving the same muscle groups. In order to combine these elements in the build-up to competition, the following exercise regime could produce an explosive performance on the day:

Sequence A

Working explosively on conventional exercises, perform 5 repetitions in 6 seconds; 5 sets per exercise, 2 warm-up, 3 intense. Exercises must be suitable for quick repetitions; full cleans will be difficult but bench press, jump squats, hang clean and push press are all suitable.

Sequence B

As sequence A, but consolidating previous work with further exercises:

1a. Bench
1b. Press-ups with clap from blocks
2a. Squat
2b. Hurdle jumps
3a. Clean
3b. Medicine ball throw
4a. Press
4b. Medicine ball throw

	Session 1	Session 2	Session 3
Week 1	A	B	A
Week 2	B	A	B
Week 3	A	B	A
Week 4	B	B	A
Week 5	B	B	A
Week 6	B	B	–

SPEED

Speed for throwing can be improved in two ways: you can become stronger so that the implement becomes relatively lighter, or you can become explosively stronger. A very specific and effective way of increasing your throwing speed is to use a light implement. As with the use of heavy implements, care must be taken not to use too light an implement since co-ordination will be affected. Try to stay within 15 per cent of the competitive weight, for example senior men should use a 6.25kg hammer.

ENDURANCE

At first glance the throwing events require little in the way of endurance. However, to reach elite levels, you must be fit enough to endure long, hard training sessions and able to reproduce quality throws time after time in order to build a good technique.

Concentrate on building endurance at the beginning of the training year (September and October) when long runs and circuit training should figure prominently in the training schedule. Following this, maintain a stamina unit within your weekly programme, whether it be a circuit, a jog or repetition strides. Like strength, stamina is relatively easy to retain but, if not practised, can be quickly lost.

Circuit Training

Circuit training is a useful way of building both strength and endurance. Choose 6 to 8 exercises that work the muscle groups required for your event. Each exercise is performed in turn for 15 seconds, with a maximum number of repetitions, followed by 30 seconds' rest until all the exercises have been completed. A longer rest is then taken (about 5 minutes) and a second set is performed. The training intensity can be altered to suit your maturity and level of fitness by:

1. Changing the number of exercises.
2. Changing the exercise time.
3. Changing the rest time.
4. Changing the number of sets.

To prevent injuries to what are, for throwers, the sensitive areas of knees and lower back, it is advisable to perform regular knee and back circuits to condition these areas. Six to eight exercises which work these areas should be chosen (hyperextensions or one-legged squats, for example) but ensure that you exercise them from every angle possible.

EXPLOSIVE STRENGTH

Weight-lifting strength is not always synonymous with throwing performance; it would certainly be a mistake to rely solely on lifting big, heavy weights in training. Other activities can produce gains in explosive strength which complement the gross strength gains of weight-lifting.

Sprinting

Moving a large frame quickly over short distances requires, and develops, explosive strength. You should be a good sprinter, if not over 100m, certainly over 30 to 60m. The most valuable strengthening phase of sprinting is the first 20m when the effort to overcome the resistance of your own weight is considerable. Flat out sprinting from a standing start should be restricted to 20 to 40m.

Jumping and Bounding
(*Figs 139 to 141*)

These activities should be included in your overall schedule all the year round to develop elastic strength. Multiple hopping and bounding requires recruitment, not only of the muscles' contractile component, but also of the elastic component of the relevant reflex mechanisms in muscle and tendon. This clearly demands a high level of co-ordination in the selective recruitment of muscle fibres. The majority of throwers are heavy and bounding activities should therefore be restricted to not more than six foot contacts. It is also advisable to ensure that the surface used has some give in it.

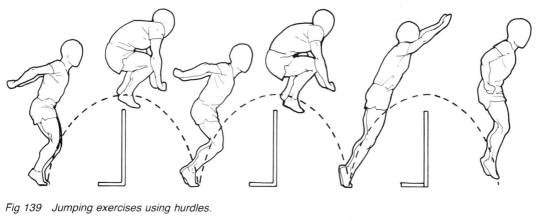

Fig 139   Jumping exercises using hurdles.

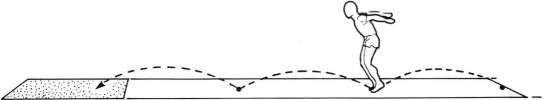

Fig 140   Jumping exercises using a
         sand pit.

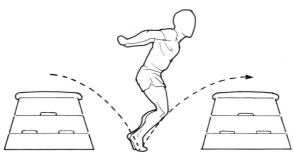

Fig 141   Jumping exercises using boxes.

Throwing

A very specific way of gaining explosive strength is by throwing heavy objects or implements. However, do not use too heavy an implement when practising event technique. As a guide no more than 10 per cent in excess of the competitive weight should be thrown (2.2kg discus for senior men for example). Should a heavier implement be used, choose a position from which the movement can be controlled, for example a standing throw. If too much weight is thrown, its usefulness to competition performance will be reduced because the movement will slow down and the required co-ordination will be different from that used in throwing a competition weight.

A superb piece of equipment for strengthening and conditioning the torso is the medicine ball. Many rotational exercises can be performed with it, both general and specific. When using the medicine ball, attempt a high number of repetitions (10 or more) and perform your movements quickly and explosively.

Exercises for Torso Strength and Conditioning

Fig 142

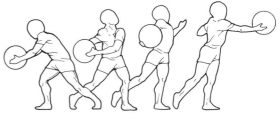

Fig 143

Fig 144

Fig 145

Fig 146

Fig 147

Fig 148

Fig 149

Fig 150

Fig 151

Fig 152

Fitness for Throwing

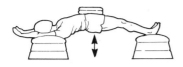

Fig 153

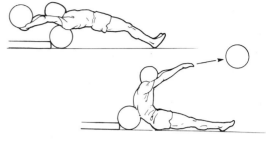

Fig 154

Fig 155

Fig 156

Fig 157

Fig 158

Fig 159

78

Depth Jumping
(Figs 160 to 162)

If a muscle is pre-stretched, such as when jumping down on to the ground, the muscle contraction will be much greater than that experienced in a conventional movement. The basic depth jumping movement involves jumping down from a platform and then exploding immediately upwards. When using depth jumping, the following principles should be adhered to:

1. The platform from which the jump is taken should not exceed 50cm; dropping from a great height will make a quick return, involving the stretch reflex, impossible.
2. Make sure that the rebound is quick and explosive.
3. Try to isolate your legs by having your hands on hips and do not assist the upward jump with your arms.
4. If you are heavy, practise depth jumping only once a week, as too frequent practise can result in muscle soreness.

Fig 160   Depth jump – start.

Fig 161   Depth jump – mid-point.

Fig 162 Depth jump – finish.

You can also perform stretch reflex exercises for the upper body, by dropping from 20cm blocks and performing press-ups explosively, for example, or by catching and immediately throwing a heavy medicine ball.

MOBILITY

In order to apply your force over as great a range as possible, you must improve your technique and ensure that your mobility is such that you can assume rangy positions.

Supple athletes are less likely to be injured in training; they have mobility beyond the normal movement range, so when a new position is assumed, to which they are unaccustomed, no injury occurs.

You will need to perform general mobility exercises every day. A convenient way of doing this is to incorporate them in your warm-up for training. Specific mobility sessions will be needed to increase, rather than simply to maintain mobility. Substantial mobility sessions in early winter will increase your range which should be easily maintained.

As with most aspects of fitness, mobility is specific to each limb; the ability to touch your toes may not help you to assume a powerful, rangy throwing position. Look at your throwing action and try to design specific throwing mobility exercises. The exercises illustrated are examples related to the throwing action.

Safety

The safest way to perform mobility work is to stretch slowly to the end of your range (the end position) and hold this stretched position for 10 seconds. Release, relax and then repeat the action up to 10 or 15 times. When holding the stretched position other parts of the body should be as relaxed as possible. Try to concentrate on relaxing the muscles which are being stretched.

TECHNIQUE

The acquisition of technique is essential if you are to throw a long way. Many hours will be spent learning the basic technique of the event and then years of technique training will be devoted to perfecting these basic skills.

Basic Exercises for Mobility in Torso and Shoulders

Fig 163

Fig 164

Fig 165

Fig 166

Fig 167

Fig 168

Fig 169

Fitness for Throwing

Fig 170

Fig 171

Fig 172

Fig 173

Fig 174

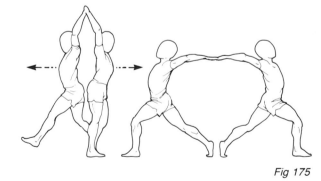

Fig 175

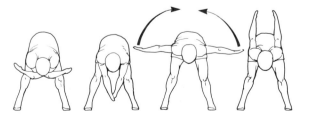

Fig 176

Fig 177

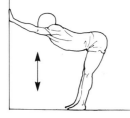

Fig 178

Fig 179

Fig 180

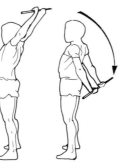

Fig 181

Fig 182

Fig 183

Fig 184

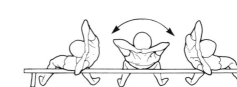

Fig 185

The old adage 'technique first, sweat second' holds good for the throwing events. The skills of the event should always be practised when you are fresh; under no circumstances should you be allowed to throw poorly due to fatigue.

Modifying Technique

At the end of the season, coach and athlete must decide which points of technique need changing. If the modifications are major, most of the technique work related to these changes must take place during the winter months. Major technique changes should always be made during the early winter period and only small refinements can be considered close to or into the season.

Conditions for technique work must be as close to perfect as possible. In the winter months this means moving indoors for net throwing or drills. Too much indoor net throwing and drill work may lead to technical problems, however; you will not be able to see the effect of your technique on the flight of the implement. It is always wise to continue to throw outside regularly.

Schedule

The total throw combines several different skills. For example, in discus they are turning balance at the back, the turn across the circle and the final sling. It is sometimes beneficial to practise part skills but they must always be brought back into the whole eventually. The closer the season is, the more the whole technique must be the prime consideration.

Winter

1. 5 partial stands
2. 10 fixed feet stands
3. 5 stop and check glides
4. 10 fixed feet glides
5. 10 full throws

Summer

1. 10 fixed feet stands
2. 5 fixed feet glides
3. 20 full throws
4. 10 full throws with a light implement

When evaluating an athlete's throwing technique, several faults may be evident; the underlying cause of these faults must be found. Often a fault is a symptom and not a cause, so you must remedy the cause and the symptoms (the faults) will disappear.

An athlete cannot think of more than one technical point at a time. A priority list of fault corrections must be made and the most important fault worked upon first. Never work on more than one technical point at a time.

7 Planning Your Training

How can the individual units of training which make a successful thrower best be incorporated into an overall training plan?

Your schedule must be formulated taking into account your ambition, maturity and personal wishes. When planning the overall schedule, the following points should be observed:

1. Time available. No schedule can be written without considering the total amount of time which you can afford to devote to training. You should endeavour to make the best use of the time allocated.

2. Facilities. These will influence, to a degree, the composition of your training schedule. You must consider such factors as the availability of weight training facilities.

3. Age and experience. It is not just a question of giving a youngster a watered down version of a world-class schedule since certain activities such as bounding and heavy overhead lifting may injure the immature frame. Even with a mature athlete, any sudden increase in volume, or substantial work in a new area may lead to injury if not carefully phased in.

4. Progression. There should be a gradual build-up of work and no sharp breaks or increases in work between the months, phases or seasons of the year.

5. Recovery. Easy days should follow hard ones, easy weeks follow hard weeks. You should not be subjected to intensive work on consecutive days since this may lead to injury and mental fatigue.

6. Variety. It is possible and advisable to include a mixture of activities on a training night. Stamina may well follow skill and strength work on a single evening.

7. Competitive aims. These should be realistic and will dictate the amount of work necessary to achieve pre-set goals for the forthcoming season.

THE NOVICE

The novice athlete's schedule is quite naturally of lower volume and intensity than that of his more experienced counterpart. The schedule at this level should be simple and without too much specialisation.

Winter

Training sessions should be three times a week.

Weekend session

1. Warm-up, followed by general mobility (20 minutes).
2. Throwing: 25 throws, subdivided into skill elements (40 minutes).
3. Second event work, hurdling for example: 5 sets of 3 flights of hurdles (20 minutes).
4. Jog 800m to warm down (5 minutes).

Midweek sessions

Session 1
1. Warm-up and mobility work (20 minutes).

2. Medicine ball work, emphasising the torso muscles and the right hip movement of throwing (20 minutes).
3. Strength circuit: general exercises (20 minutes).

Session 2
1. Warm-up and mobility work (20 minutes).
2. Skill drills, indoors (30 minutes).
3. Strength circuit: emphasis on torso muscles (20 minutes).

Summer

Training sessions should be four times a week.

Weekend session

1. Warm-up, including mobility exercises (10 minutes).
2. Throwing: 30 throws; 10 standing, 10 full, 10 with a light implement (40 minutes).
3. Sprinting: drills, then 4 × 30m (20 minutes).
4. Continuous relay for endurance (10 minutes).

Midweek

Session 1
1. Warm-up (10 minutes).
2. Throwing: 15 throws; 5 standing, 10 full (20 minutes).
3. Long jumps: drills, then 5 × 5 stride jumps (20 minutes).
4. Medicine ball work (15 minutes).
5. Endurance work: 800m fartlek (10 minutes).

Session 2
1. Warm-up (10 minutes).
2. Second throwing event work: 20 throws

(30 minutes).
3. Hurdling: 5 × 4 flights of hurdles (15 minutes).
4. Mobility sessions (15 minutes).
5. Jog warm down: 1200m (10 minutes).

Session 3
1. Warm-up (10 minutes).
2. Throwing session: 15 throws for distance (20 minutes).
3. Acceleration runs: 4 × 60m (15 minutes).
4. Mini circuit: 5 exercises, 2 sets (10 minutes).
5. Jog warm down (10 minutes).

While you mature and progress, the basic winter and summer format will remain the same. Increasingly you will specialise, though, and will devote more time to strength training as your physique develops. Eventually more detailed planning of the training year will be required: simply to divide the year into two (winter and summer) will not suffice if your full potential is to be realised.

ADVANCED SCHEDULE
(*Figs 186 & 187*)

To achieve success at national and international levels it is essential to subdivide the whole athletic year into a preparation phase, a competition phase and a transition phase. The long preparation phase (6 to 7 months) lays a firm foundation for the competition phase (4 to 5 months) and allows form to peak. The athletic year progresses gradually from general work to the specific, and from large quantities to quality; lots of general work in the depths of winter tapering to specific, high quality, low volume work in the competitive period.

Months	Nov	Dec	Jan	Feb	Mar	Apr	May	June	July	Aug	Sep	Oct
Phases	1				2		3		4		5	
Periods	Prep						Comp					Trans

Fig 186 Single periodised year.

Months	Nov	Dec	Jan	Feb	Mar	Apr	May	June	July	Aug	Sep	Oct
Phases	1^1	2^1	3^1			1^2	2^2	3^2	4		5	
Periods	Prep		Comp		Prep			Comp				Trans

Fig 187 Double periodised year.

Dividing the year into phases is called periodisation; it is possible to use double periodisation or single periodisation.

For athletes such as shot putters double periodisation satisfies the need for having two competitive phases in the year (indoor and outdoor) and, with constant changes of emphasis, it certainly avoids both staleness and boredom. Double periodisation can also be used for the long throwers (discus, hammer and javelin) who may not compete in winter but who could still peak for high quality training throws or control tests.

One advantage of single periodisation is that the long preparation phase ensures that a sound fitness base is achieved; an injury in the second preparation phase of a double periodised year could leave the athlete woefully short of conditioning for the summer competitive season.

Whichever periodisation options you choose, the phases are tackled in the same manner.

Early Preparation Phase ($1-1^1-1^2$)

Here the emphasis is on conditioning or 'training to train'. The repetitions are high and the volume great, but the intensity is low: 150m of strides, sets of 10 repetitions with weights, circuits, mobility sessions etc. The work tends not to be specific; many exercises are performed with the aim of building up the whole of the muscular system. This early phase is gradually modified to become the second stage.

Second Preparation Phase ($2-2^1-2^2$)

This could be termed the strength phase, with volume kept high but intensity greatly increased. The work tends towards activities specific to events: much more throwing and related exercises. The intensity of this phase can often cause a temporary drop in throwing performance.

SAMPLE SCHEDULE

	Phase 1 (Nov–Feb)	Phase 2 (Mar–May)
Strength	Initially 3 sets of 8 to 12 repetitions of many exercises (6 weeks); reducing repetitions to 5 to 8 and increasing the number of sets but reducing the number of exercises: squat, clean, bench press, and their variations. Work three times each week.	A mixture of few repetitions (3 to 5) and pyramid work. Exercises: few, but added to the basic power exercises (squats, cleans, press) are specialised exercises. Shot: incline dumbell press. Discus: bent arm flying. Javelin: bent arm pullover; French press. Hammer: disc circling. Work three times each week.
Specific Strength	Initially minimal but phased in will be work with overweight implements. Shot: standing 8kg shot. Discus: standing 2.5kg disc; full 2.2kg disc. Javelin: weighted ball throw; no run up. Hammer: short wire, 10kg. Work twice each week.	Work continues but the weights are closer to the competitive weight to allow full technique throws. Work twice each week.
Explosive Strength	Bounding: javelin up to 5 foot contacts; heavy throws up to 3 foot contacts. Once each week. Medicine ball work: javelin, three times each week. Lots of sets and repetitions to condition the throwing muscles; heavy throws: twice each week, emphasising torso muscles.	Bounding: javelin 2 to 3 foot contacts; heavy throws, standing jumps. Twice each week. Medicine ball work: reduced repetitions, increased weight and intensity. Javelin: three times each week. Heavy throws: twice each week.
Running	Initially one 4,000m run each week plus one 150m strides session, phasing down to one stride session (100m × 6) and one 90 per cent sprint session (60m × 6).	Sprints: 30 to 60 metres, twice each week. Javelin: greater volume, three times each week.
Technique	One technique session each week using standard weight.	One session each week.
Mobility	In the first half of the phase mobility sessions are emphasised to increase range of movement.	Mobility is a regular part of the training week.

Fig 188   Advanced schedule, single periodisation for male athletes.

Phase 3 (May–June)	Phase 4 (July–Aug)	Phase 5 (Aug–Sept)
Weights performed faster with reduced loadings, for example 5 repetitions maximum with 85% of normal loadings. Volume decreases. Exercises are explosive: jump squat, snatch, fast bench press, push press. Specialised exercises continue. Work one to two times a week.	Volume increased but the weights still handled explosively. The aim is to maintain strength, not increase it. Work two to three times each week.	As phase 3.
Little or no overweight work.	Return to overweight work for first half of the phase; no more than a 10 per cent increase.	As phase 3
Bounding reduced to a minimum; if performed, high quality, few sets. Medicine ball work: one session each week, low intensity, low volume.	Quality bounding twice each week. Quality, low volume medicine ball work twice each week.	As phase 3
Work kept short and sharp, 5 × 30m timed sprints for example. Once a week.	Increased to twice a week.	As phase 3
Heavy throws: 3 to 4 sessions each week mixing in light implement work. Javelin: 2 to 3 sessions.	3 to 4 sessions, working on technique points observed in Phase 3.	As phase 3
As phase 2	As phase 2	As phase 3

Competition Phase (3–5–3¹–3²)

The aim in all earlier phases is to prepare you to throw the implement as far from your front foot as possible. To reach this objective you must reserve much of your available energy for throwing, with the emphasis on quick, light, fast work of low volume.

Second Competition Phase (4)

It is impossible to maintain peak performance for months on end; four to five weeks is often as long as you will be able to maintain a high standard of performance. To enable you to peak later in the season it is necessary to undergo a block of work that is similar to that of the preparation phase. The intensity should be reduced and the volume increased, although not to the levels of the winter preparation period.

Transition Phase

This is a period of active recovery. Initially, at the end of the competitive season, a short rest should be taken followed by a change of exercise: swimming, soccer, basketball or squash for example. This is an important phase which recharges the batteries both physically and mentally.

Individual Session

Several fitness units can be included in a single session but you must ensure that it follows a logical pattern, for example:

1. *Warm-up*
800m jog.
3 × 60m strides.
General mobility exercises.
Specific mobility exercises.
2 or 3 easy throws.
2. *Technique work*
10 standing throws, fixed feet.
15 full throws.
10 throws, light implement.
3. *Fitness work*
6 sets of standing triple jump.
10 sets of standing long jump.
6 × 30m timed sprints.
4. *Warm down*
Short stretching session.
Jog 600m.

This format never changes: warm-up, technique work, fitness work, warm down. It is important to warm up and to perform technique work when fresh.

8 Evaluating the Athlete

Athletics is a series of tests and measurements; measuring the athlete's performance helps to evaluate him. These tests and measurements are a valuable tool for both coach and athlete since they can help to formulate a training schedule by:

1. Diagnosing weaknesses and strengths.
2. Measuring improvement.
3. Assessing the success of a training programme.
4. Assessing the speed at which the athlete improves.
5. Predicting future performances.
6. Giving confidence.
7. Providing motivation.
8. Giving a warning of staleness and the possible onset of injury.

When using tests the coach or athlete should progress through the following stages:

1. Test the athlete and look for weaknesses in comparison with other athletes. To do this you should have an idea of what is a good–average–poor performance for that particular test.
2. Formulate a schedule to eradicate these weaknesses.
3. Perform the training and complete the schedule.
4. Re-test the athlete and evaluate his status compared with the initial test. Are the weaknesses beginning to disappear?
5. Using the results of the tests, make modifications to the schedule.

These stages are repeated and the athlete is assured of a balanced, progressive development.

CHOOSING TESTS

The problem is often making a choice from a vast array of tests available. Before making your final choice, you must ensure that:

1. The test is valid, that is that it measures what it sets out to measure. Is a 30m sprint a test of speed?
2. It must be reliable and capable of constant repetition.
3. It must be objective, so that if two coaches were to test in the same way, they would obtain the same results.
4. It must be simple and easy to carry out.
5. You should be able to gauge strengths and weaknesses from the test: is a 1.10m vertical jump good? You should be in a position to draw up a scale of scores ranging from 'excellent' down to 'very poor'.

There are many hundreds of tests that can be used and you should analyse the requirements of the event to determine which characteristics are necessary for top performances and then choose or devise the test best suited to measure these factors. Once you have formulated a set of tests, you must use them in a planned manner, usually testing at the start of the winter period and thereafter at regular intervals.

The coach administering tests and measurements must ask the question 'Can this test teach me something that will ultimately help athletic performance?' If the answer is yes, then the evaluation of data obtained is the vital last stage. After analysing the results, the coach must draw conclusions and decide what changes are to be made. Intelligent use of tests and sound evaluation of their use will maximise the progress of an athlete.

TEST QUADRATHLON

The Test Quadrathlon comprises the most popular battery of tests used by throwers. Athletes have three attempts at each event.

Standing Long Jump

With your feet over the edge of the sand pit, crouch, lean forward, swing your arms backward, then jump horizontally as far as possible, from both feet, into the sand pit. Measure to the nearest point of contact.

Three Jumps

Starting with feet comfortably apart and toes just behind the take-off mark, take three continuous two-footed jumps into the sand pit.

30m Sprint

On the starter's signal, sprint from a stationary set position, as fast as possible, to the finish line. The timekeeper stands at the finish and times the run from the moment your foot contacts the ground on the first running stride to the moment when your torso crosses the line. Spikes are allowed.

Fig 189   Standing long jump, starting with the feet over the edge of the sand pit.

Fig 190   The three jump sequence must be continuous.

Fig 192 Start position for the overhead shot.

Fig 191 The 30 metre sprint, timed from the first foot contact.

Overhead Shot Throw

Stand on the shot stopboard facing away from the landing area, with your feet a comfortable distance apart. The shot is held cupped in both hands. Crouch, lowering the shot between your legs, then drive upwards to cast the shot back over your head. There is no penalty for following through but you must land feet first. Measurements are taken from the inside edge of the stopboard. Implement weights are as set down by the Amateur Athletic Association.

Fig 193 Midway through the overhead shot.

Points	3 Jumps	S.L.J.	30m	O.H.Shot	Points	3 Jumps	S.L.J.	30m	O.H.Shot
100	10.98	3.68	3.22	20.80					
99	10.92	3.66	3.24	.68	69	9.12	3.06	3.76	17.08
98	10.86	3.64	3.26	.56	68	9.06	3.04	3.77	.96
97	10.80	3.62	3.28	.44	67	9.00	3.02	3.79	.84
96	10.74	3.60	3.30	.32	66	8.94	3.00	3.80	.72
95	10.68	3.58	3.32	.20	65	8.88	2.98	3.82	.60
94	10.62	3.56	3.34	20.08	64	8.82	2.96	3.84	.48
93	10.56	3.54	3.36	.96	63	8.76	2.94	3.85	.36
92	10.50	3.52	3.38	.84	62	8.70	2.92	3.87	.24
91	10.44	3.50	3.40	.72	61	8.64	2.90	3.88	.12
90	10.38	3.48	3.42	19.60 90	60	8.58	2.88	3.90	16.00 60
89	10.32	3.46	3.44	.48	59	8.52	2.86	3.91	.88
88	10.26	3.44	3.46	.36	58	8.46	2.84	3.93	.76
87	10.20	3.42	3.48	.24	57	8.40	2.82	3.94	.64
86	10.14	3.40	3.50	.12	56	8.34	2.80	3.95	.52
85	10.08	3.38	3.51	19.00	55	8.28	2.78	3.97	.40
84	10.02	3.36	3.52	.88	54	8.22	2.76	3.98	.28
83	9.96	3.34	3.54	.76	53	8.16	2.74	4.00	.16
82	9.90	3.32	3.55	.64	52	8.10	2.72	4.01	15.04
81	9.84	3.30	3.57	.52	51	8.04	2.70	4.03	.92
80	9.78	3.28	3.59	18.40 80	50	7.98	2.68	4.04	14.80 50
79	9.72	3.26	3.60	.28	49	7.92	2.66	4.05	.65
78	9.66	3.24	3.62	.16	48	7.86	2.64	4.06	.50
77	9.60	3.22	3.64	18.04	47	7.80	2.62	4.08	.35
76	9.54	3.20	3.65	.92	46	7.74	2.60	4.09	.20
75	9.48	3.18	3.67	.80	45	7.68	2.58	4.10	14.05
74	9.42	3.16	3.68	.68	44	7.62	2.56	4.12	.90
73	9.36	3.14	3.69	.56	43	7.56	2.54	4.13	.75
72	9.30	3.12	3.71	.44	42	7.50	2.52	4.15	.60
71	9.24	3.10	3.73	.32	41	7.44	2.50	4.16	.45
70	9.18	3.08	3.74	17.20 70	40	7.38	2.48	4.19	13.30 40

Fig 194   Points awarded according to performance in the test quadrathlon.

Points	3 Jumps	S.L.J.	30m	O.H.Shot		Points	3 Jumps	S.L.J.	30m	O.H.Shot	
39	7.32	2.46	4.20	.15		19	6.12	2.06	4.50	.15	
38	7.26	2.44	4.21	13.00		18	6.06	2.04	4.51	10.00	
37	7.20	2.42	4.23	.85		17	6.00	2.02	4.52	.85	
36	7.14	2.40	4.24	.70		16	5.94	2.00	4.54	.70	
35	7.08	2.38	4.25	.55		15	5.88	1.98	4.55	.55	
34	7.02	2.36	4.27	.40		14	5.82	1.96	4.57	.40	
33	6.96	2.34	4.28	.25		13	5.76	1.94	4.59	.25	
32	6.90	2.32	4.30	12.10		12	5.70	1.92	4.61	9.10	
31	6.84	2.30	4.32	.95		11	5.64	1.90	4.63	.95	
30	6.78	2.28	4.33	11.80	30	10	5.58	1.88	4.65	8.80	10
29	6.72	2.26	4.35	.65		9	5.50	1.86	4.67	.60	
28	6.66	2.24	4.36	.50		8	5.42	1.84	4.69	.40	
27	6.60	2.22	4.38	.35		7	5.36	1.82	4.71	.20	
26	6.54	2.20	4.39	.20		6	5.26	1.80	4.73	8.00	
25	6.48	2.18	4.40	11.05		5	5.18	1.77	4.75	.80	
24	6.42	2.16	4.42	.90		4	5.10	1.74	4.78	.60	
23	6.36	2.14	4.43	.75		3	5.02	1.71	4.80	.40	
22	6.30	2.12	4.45	.60		2	4.94	1.68	4.82	.20	
21	6.24	2.10	4.46	.45		1	4.86	1.65	4.85	7.00	0pts
20	6.18	2.08	4.48	10.30	20						

Additional Points

3 Jumps : 1 point extra for each 6cm above 10.98.
S.L.J. : 1 point for each 2cm above 3.68.
30m : 1 point for each 0.02 below 3.22.
O.H.Shot : 1 point for each 12cm above 20.80.

Appendix Barrier Breakers

Records are made to be broken! Hardly a year passes without a record being broken, although some records last longer than others. Distances, especially those composed of round numbers, act as barriers which often prove hard to beat. Once broken, many other athletes quickly follow and the achievement becomes commonplace. However, a place in athletics' history should be set aside for those first barrier breakers.

DISCUS

Men

Barrier Broken

40m	40.72	M. Sheridan	(USA)	1902
45m	47.58	J. Duncan	(USA)	1912
50m	51.03	E. Krenz	(USA)	1930
55m	55.33	A. Consolini	(Ita)	1948
60m	60.56	J. Silvester	(USA)	1961
200ft (60.96m)	61.10	A. Oerter	(USA)	1962
65m	65.22	L. Danek	(Cze)	1965
70m	70.24	M. Wilkins	(USA)	1976

Women

Barrier Broken

40m	40.35	J. Wajsowna	(Pol)	1932
45m	45.53	G. Mauermayer	(Ger)	1935
50m	50.50	N. Dumbadze	(USSR)	1952
55m	57.04	N. Dumbadze	(USSR)	1952
60m	61.26	L. Westermann	(FRG)	1967
200ft (60.96m)	61.26	L. Westermann	(FRG)	1967
65m	65.42	F. Melnik	(USSR)	1972
70m	70.20	F. Melnik	(USSR)	1975

SHOT

Men

Barrier Broken

16m	16.04	Emil Hirschfeld	(Ger)	1928
17m	17.04	Jack Torrance	(USA)	1934
18m	18.00	Parry O'Brien	(USA)	1953
60ft (18.29m)	18.42	Parry O'Brien	(USA)	1954
19m	19.06	Parry O'Brien	(USA)	1956
20m	20.06	Bill Nieder	(USA)	1960
21m	21.05	Randy Matson	(USA)	1965
70ft (21.33m)	21.52	Randy Matson	(USA)	1965
22m	22.00	Alex Baryshnikov	(USSR)	1976

*Brian Oldfield, as a professional, exceeded 22 metres several times in 1975 with a season's best of 22.86 metres.

Women

Barrier Broken

16m	16.20	Galina Zybina	(USSR)	1953
17m	17.25	Tamara Press	(USSR)	1959
18m	18.55	Tamara Press	(USSR)	1962
60ft (18.29m)	as above			
19m	19.07	Margitta Gummel	(GDR)	1968
20m	20.09	Nadyezhda Chizhova	(USSR)	1967
21m	21.03	Nadyezhda Chizhova	(USSR)	1972
22m	22.32	Helena Fibingerova		1977

HAMMER

Barrier Broken	**Men**			
40m	40.54	James Mitchell	(USA)	1886
50m	50.01	John Flanagan	(USA)	1899
60m	60.34	Jozsef Csermak	(Hun)	1952
200ft(60.96m)	61.25	Sverre Strandli	(Nor)	1952
70m	70.33	Hal Connolly	(USA)	1960
80m	80.14	Boris Zaychuk	(USSR)	1978

Appendix

JAVELIN

Men

Barrier Broken

60m	60.64	Mor Koczan	(Hun)	1911
200ft(60.96m)	61.45	Juho Saaristo	(Fin)	1912
70m	71.01	Erik Lundqvist	(Swe)	1928
80m	80.41	Bud Held	(USA)	1953
300ft(91.44m)	91.72	Terje Pedersen	(Nor)	1964
100m	104.80	Uwe Hohn	(GDR)	1984

*In 1986 the specifications for the men's 800g javelin were changed and the progression of javelin world records ended when the first of the new specification javelin records was set.

Women

Barrier Broken

60m				
200ft(60.96m)	61.38	Elvira Ozolina	(USSR)	1964
70m	70.08	Tatyana Biryulina	(USSR)	1980

Useful Addresses

British Amateur Athletic Board
Francis House
Francis Street
London SW1P 1DL

The BAAB Coaching Office, Amateur Athletic Association and Women's Amateur Athletic Association can all be found at the above address.

Midland Counties AAA
Devonshire House
Deritend
Birmingham B12 0LP

Northern AAA
Studio 44
Bluecoat Chambers
School Lane
Liverpool L1 3BX

Southern AAA
Francis House
Francis Street
London SW1P 1DL

Welsh AAA
54 Charles Street
Cardiff CF1 4EF

Scottish AAA
16 Royal Crescent
Glasgow G3 7SL

Northern Ireland AAA
20 Kernan Park
Portadown
County Armagh

IAAF
3 Hans Crescent
Knightsbridge
London SW1X 0LN

International Athletes Club
210 High Holborn
London WC1V 7BW

Index

Crowood Sports Books

*	**Badminton** – The Skills of the Game	*Peter Roper*
	Basketball – The Skills of the Game	*Paul Stimpson*
*	**Canoeing** – Skills and Techniques	*Neil Shave*
*	**The Skills of Cricket**	*Keith Andrew*
	Endurance Running	*Norman Brook*
*	**Fitness for Sport**	*Rex Hazeldine*
*	**Golf** – The Skills of the Game	*John Stirling*
	Hockey – The Skills of the Game	*John Cadman*
	Judo – Skills and Techniques	*Tony Reay*
	Jumping	*Malcolm Arnold*
	Rugby Union – The Skills of the Game	*Barrie Corless*
	Skiing – Developing Your Skill	*John Shedden*
	Sprinting and Hurdling	*Peter Warden*
	Squash – The Skills of the Game	*Ian McKenzie*
	Swimming	*John Verrier*
	Table Tennis – The Skills of the Game	*Gordon Steggall*
	Tennis – The Skills of the Game	*Bill Moss*
	Throwing	*Max Jones*
	Volleyball – The Skills of the Game	*Keith Nicholls*
	Windsurfing – Improving Techniques	*Ben Oakley*

* **Also available in paperback**

**Further details of titles available or in preparation
can be obtained from the publishers.**